INHALANT ADDICTION

"The Silent Epidemic"

DR. SANJEEV PRASAD

Notion Press

Old No. 38, New No. 6
McNichols Road, Chetpet
Chennai - 600 031

First Published by Notion Press 2018

ISBN 978-1-64429-616-5

CONTENTS

PREFACE

For a professional who has worked in the field of addiction and de-addiction for more than three decades it has been a period full of challenges, satisfactions and deep anguish. I have worked hard as a psychiatrist and adopted various roles such as a grass root worker, an awareness generation worker, head of de-addiction centers and protocol designers for international projects on drug abuse.

Each day in the field brings in something new, some new knowledge, something you were not aware of in the past. Every addict has the same story of devastation to tell but each case is different and unique in details and in the foot prints of misfortunes it leaves behind.

The field of addiction and de-addiction has always been intriguing and full of challenge.

It is with great pleasure that I am writing the foreword to this book. We have had books on addictions in the past. These books have discussed nicotine dependence, alcoholism, cannabis and opiates. It is true that much attention has been given to these addictions as they are visibly affecting the health of many people and the society. They have been an immense financial burden on the health delivery system as well.

Lot of revenue goes into research and designing of new molecules for treatment of the mentioned addictions. Significant amount also goes into designing awareness programs. With all the finances from the government, NGOs and the efforts of those who matter we have crossed new milestones daily. We have made advances in diagnosing, treating and preventing drug addiction. However it is disheartening to see that certain covert addictions which are silently spreading across all sections of the society are getting ignored despite their lethal effects on the addict.

There was never a health issue of a large scale addiction faced by us therefore private practitioners and government hospitals could tackle it at their own level in the best possible way they knew. The government was not involved in a big way except for the usual healthcare that it provides through budget, planning and policies. Thus when an addiction of an epidemic proportion came along we were caught absolutely unaware, inadequately equipped and poorly prepared.

A proper protocol for treating addictions came in!to being only during such epidemics of drug abuse. During these epidemics society has witnessed large number of individuals falling prey and becoming victims of a particular drug of abuse. The book traces all such known epidemics witnessed by mankind across the globe. Specific epidemics of drug abuse which affected the Indian populace have been detailed to understand how it made its way into the society.

The book also deals with the unfolding of events which led to the development of a better health delivery system for the addicts.

The times were such when the health delivery system was thrown out of gear in the face of an urgent crisis. The addictions were rampant and the government was suddenly overwhelmed. All the departments came into an immediate action and emphasis on awareness, prevention, diagnosis and treatment evolved. Law and enforcement too came into overdrive and laws were formulated and strict actions prescribed. The enforcement too became vigilant. Thus the whole machinery came out successful with properly co-ordinated efforts and over a decade the drug abuse showed a decline though newer drugs came up. But we had a definite protocol for treatment and prevention devised by us now.

As covert addictions are largely ignored it spells a grim picture. These are potentially more harmful and dangerous. One such example is the addiction to inhalants (organic solvents). This addiction is vastly undetected as the addicts are not identifiable obviously in the earlier days. Tragically it is the children, teenagers and adolescents who are the vulnerable population.

The awareness, research, literature and treatment of these specific addictions are inadequate. The funding by the government for these addictions is negligible. The spate of this addiction has caught parents, schools, society and the administration off guard. Treatment for inhalant abuse has evolved but law and enforcement are still at a loss for making a perfect plan to combat this menace.

The book deals with the intricate issues of inhalant abuse in details. It gives detailed account of the inhalant addiction in the real world and this would be very helpful for people who wish to seek guidance or treatment for their next of kin.

A successfully treated drug addict means an individual has recovered and a family has been saved. For every individual drug dependent treated there are at least four normal members of their family whose quality of life has improved.

I am sure after reading the book you would be much more aware, prepared and well guided on the awareness, prevention and treatment of inhalant addictions.

INTRODUCTION

RECREATIONAL ACTIVITIES

Recreational activities have always been an inseparable part of the humans ever since he set his foot on the earth. Since the prehistoric times the humans have yearned for enjoyment. Prancing around in the safe limits of his habitat the wilderness; savoring what he had hunted, making love and maybe having invented some games, these being the usual enjoyment he would have looked for.

Wish I could travel in time and see what our ancestors did for enjoyment. You could run your imagination to any length. Chasing each other, climbing the big trees, riding a domesticated animal, racing each other must have brought the thrills that make one happy. Wrestling could have been the games and recreation of those times. But survival was the most important primary concern and therefore all attention was for securing himself and his commune, his family. Tools weapons for hunting and guarding oneself took much of the imagination and therefore much less time was left for fun.

When the humans started living in communities and experimented with farming they identified the plants good for them. Security was more permanent now and more leisure time put the humans onto many recreational activities as cave paintings, kayaking, pottery, war games, hunting (this was only for food in the past),spiritual ceremonies.

The experience of drug/alcohol must have been serendipity, a chance discovery which gave the human a thrill not experienced before. It would be shared by others in times to come and thus a drug taking behavior to get a high would be accepted as one way of enjoying by the community. Many would still venture further out to try other related or unrelated things as plants, fruits, mushrooms etc. to get a desired mind altering high.

HISTORY OF ADDICTIONS IN HUMANS

Ever wonder how long people have been hooked on mind-altering drugs?

History of Addiction in the Indian Subcontinent

Rig Veda is the most ancient and elaborates literature available to us on this subject. There are many passages in the ancient Sanskrit texts that provide information on the intoxications used by our ancestors of bygone days. In the Rig Veda Samhita there are hymns which show that "soma (wine) was kept in leather bottles and freely sold to all comers." It may be added that soma was freely consumed. Many passages in the Rig Veda are dedicated to the praise of soma. This liquor was afterward incorporated with the worship of soma – the moon god.

Elaborate rules for the preparation of this intoxicating liquor are still to be found, which shows the respect that the liquor had on the elite – if not the common people. The chosen few who partake of it give most vivid expression to the state of exaltation, of intensified vitality, which raises them above the level of humanity."

It is interesting to study how the ancient Tamils used the intoxicants. Much of this information can be gleaned from the ancient Tamil literature of the Sangam age. They are various anthologies belonging to the 2nd century AD. These drinks are called kal and given various names pizhi, theral, ariyal, naravu, and mattu depending upon how they are produced, by squeezing, filtering, etc. The varieties are those obtained from the coconut tree, palmyra palm, and date palm; some varieties were obtained from the fruits like jackfruit; some from honey; and others were "manufactured" from rice and other cereals. It is not possible to decide how intoxicating they were some must have been very potent indeed.

According to researchers the drink was part of the cuisine and freely used by both sexes and all classes of people. Many a time the drinks were offered during social intercourse. The habit, needless to say, was prevalent in the courts of the royalties and various chieftains and was freely indulged in by the royalty and the various visitors and guests.

In another reference, a courageous and bold warrior is offered the drink in the form of *kalangal,* probably a cocktail, superior in quality offered to him by the king, who himself takes the inferior, less potent, and plain *"theral".*

In another incident, the "dutiful" daughter offers cooked *viraal* fish to her father who is intoxicated with the drink *"theral".*

References are also there of offering "kal" to the poetess by the chieftain. [1]

Cannabis in India has been used since as early as 3000 BCE (rough estimate). In Indian society, common terms for cannabis preparations include charas (resin), ganja (dried leaves, inflorescence), and bhang (seeds and leaves). A milkshake made from bhang is one of the most common licit usages of cannabis in India.

Cannabis was used for recreation, ceremonial, and meditative purposes. Bhang was traditionally used in festivals, and Ganja (Grass), Charas (Hashish) was smoked for recreation, meditation.

History of Intoxication in Other Parts of the World

According to a newly published reports based on decades of intense and laborious archaeological research, humans worldwide have been using psychoactive substances like opium, alcohol and "magic mushrooms" since prehistoric times.

Humans gained knowledge about drug plants and intoxicating drinks and also ways of consuming them. They later even perfected this art of fermenting cereals, sugar, fruits to process their drink. There was exchange of information, experimentation and many new intoxicants were made. There is evidence of regular uninterrupted use of intoxicants over the centuries, and the relationship that began in prehistoric times has continued into the present day.

Now that is a "TRIP ". The high that started for humans is ever present with him.

Many researchers have carried out extensive work on the patterns of intoxicants use in the world in the pre-historic times. Very interesting data have come up which I shall summarize soon.

Since there have been no written records to provide evidence for drug use thousands of years ago, scientists have analyzed ancient remains like the fossils of psychoactive plants, the residues of alcohol and other psychoactive chemicals in vessels used to consume them or store them. The prehistoric drawings unravel some aspects of drug taking in those times.

Additionally many archaeological records have been studied to understand the cultures of intoxication consumption in pre-historic times. The data supported the theory that mind altering intoxicants were regularly used in pre-historic times. (Research by Dr Elisa Guerra-Doce, Associate professor of pre-history at university of Valladolid, Spain study in pre historic Eurasia).

In Henan province of China the remnants of a drink of fermented rice, honey and grapes was found in the earthen pots. As per scientific estimates this form of Alcohol could well have been used in the period dating around 7000 B.C.

Historical data indicating the use of hallucinogen plants in the Americas is abundant. Ancient civilizations as Incas, Aztecs and other native Indians of these regions had a culturally accepted use of "power plants" in ceremonies and spiritual practices.

The fossil remains of the hallucinogenic cactus "Peyote "was found in a cave in Peru, dating back to 8000 B.C. The seeds of mescal beans a very potent hallucinogen similar to LSD (lysergic acid di ethyl amide) in its action was found in southern Texas and northern Mexico, dating back from the end of the ninth millennium B.C. to 1000 A.D.

Evidence has been found that Intoxicating mushrooms have been used by the natives of Guatemala, Mexico, Honduras and El Salvador. The mushrooms containing Psilocybin is a very potent hallucinogen and has been used in sacred cults between? 500 B.C. and 900 A.D.

Opium: The earliest found fossilized remains of the opium plant, dating back to the mid-sixth millennium B.C., were found at an archeological site in Italy some 20 miles northwest of Rome. Remains of poppy seed capsules and traces of opiates have been discovered in the plaque and bones of human skeletons dating back to the 4th millennium B.C., along with prehistoric art showing parts of the poppy being used in religious ceremonies.

Coca leaves: The Latin name for cocoa—Theobroma—literally means, "Food of the gods." This valuable crop played an important role in many ancient South American cultures.

In its earliest forms, the Mayans used cocoa to create a ritual beverage that was shared during betrothal and marriage ceremonies, providing one of the first known links between chocolate and romance.

The earliest evidence of humans chewing coca dates back to these South America civilizations around 8,000 years ago. The remains of pieces of coca leaves have been found in house floors in Peru, and in human dental remains and mummy hair. [2]

Tobacco: The history of smoking dates back to as early as 4000 BC in the Americas in shamanistic rituals. Smoking pipes have been found in northwestern Argentina dating back to nearly 2500 B.C. There seems a possibility of these pipes being used for smoking locally available hallucinogenic plants.

EPIDEMICS OF DRUG ABUSE IN HISTORY

Intoxicants had always been a good escape from daily stresses and also part of celebrations and rituals in human history to the present times. They have held a place of importance in our society and our everyday lives.

However the same intoxicant has proved very disastrous for societies where it's use has become unbridled and unchecked. In such societies it has consumed the lives of innumerable individuals thus crippling their lives and making the society where they live in, a sick one. Such societies do not show progress but are on the decline with eroded social norms, weakened social fabric and poor economics.

From far of history to the current times we have witnessed people getting addicted to intoxicants in very large numbers. There have been epidemics of drug addictions that many societies have suffered. And there are many epidemics that are plaguing people in large numbers even today.

I am briefly discussing these epidemics with you as they give us a picture of the large scale to which the drugs can harm a society.

OPIUM EPIDEMIC

The opium trade yielded enormous profits to the British imperialists during the nineteenth century and the first half of the twentieth century. While China was forcibly converted into the largest market for opium by the British from the early nineteenth century, India emerged as a fertile ground for the cultivation of poppy and manufacturing of opium under British monopoly during the colonial period. British rule in India and British control of the Indian princely states ensured a steady supply of opium from India to China, thereby facilitating the transfer of economic surplus from China to Britain.

The Ming Dynasty of China had earlier placed a ban on the smoking of tobacco in the 17ᵗʰ century, the country began a long "love affair" with opium. Opium abuse and addiction remained a problem in the country for centuries. Throughout the 18ᵗʰ and 19ᵗʰ centuries, China struggled with widespread opium addiction The government took very serious actions as by the beginning of 20ᵗʰ century China had started growing its own opium up to 22000 tons and it had also imported huge quantities to feed the addict population which was in millions by now. Awareness committees were formed which helped people with addiction and also gave message to the masses, Traders who gave up opium trade were given respect by the society. Punishing people who did not comply and stringent laws helped contain the problem. By 1956 the government of Peoples Republic of China had virtually eliminated the problem, Chinese immigrants moved to other countries (including the United States) they brought the drug with them – thus paving the way for the smuggling routes. The USA to this day is putting up with a severe problem of OPIATE dependence on a large scale as addiction to opium and prescription drugs misuse continue. This is the Opioid Epidemic or Opioid crisis when there is a rapid increase in use of these drugs.

Canada and many European countries too are under the grip of OPIOID crisis.

India to this day is the biggest cultivat or and supplier of licit (legal) opium to the world. It is however flanked by countries as Pakistan, Afghanistan and Myanmar which are the biggest cultivator of illicit (illegal) opium. This is smuggled to Europe, USA, and other countries. It is this opium smuggling which rakes in over surplus money which is used by terrorist across the world to procure guns, ammunitions and explosives for their nefarious activities.

Some of this illicit opium finds a market in India by the drug lords for smuggling further to other countries or sell it to local drug lords who use it for preparing other drugs as morphine, heroin, and smack. Though India has been exposed to huge opium cultivation in the country(both licit and illicit) and illicit opium from neighboring countries for nearly two centuries no epidemic have been documented as was witnessed in China.

Opium has not taken epidemic proportion in India but (and it is a big BUT) it is endemic in many parts of India.

There are around 12 different tribes in Nagaland. A certain tribe has been particularly aggressive and well developed for years. They had independence in 1947 but before that, in the 1940s, British colonialists were in the region. The British wanted to develop relationships with this tribe, as they felt threatened, so they introduced opium to the community as a way to establish that relationship and to pacify them. In the process they managed to get some people addicted to opium. Over a period of months with a regular supply of opium more and more villagers became harmless drug addicts and were no longer a threat to the British. The British's job was done and what was to follow after the British left, was the tragic end of a valiant tribe and a village of opium addicts.

It's nearly three quarters of a century the tribal village is ravaged with an opium endemic. One in every three people takes opium.

The disruption in the family structure is devastating. That's probably the most prolific effect of endemic drug addiction. The model was that men would do a lot of the hard work of hunting and cutting down the forests. Nowadays, women wake up very early and go to the fields and they come back around 6 pm to look after their kids and make dinner.

Another example is of few villages in Rajasthan where taking opium is a tradition. Thus opium is served in festivals and ceremonies. In a particular village it is customary to drink opium. Opium water is poured into the hands of an elder and the guest or others drink from the hands of the elder. The mood of the guest and the host is one of merry making.

Another tribe in Rajasthan is an example where opium is used in day to day life culturally and socially. The tribe found in the northern part of Thar Desert follows a religion related to society, hygiene, bio-diversity and God. The religious group follows Sanatan Dharma and Islam principles. The sect observes a personal set of commandments with reverence for nature at its core.

In the early part of the twentieth century some states in India had issued permits to opium addicts. With this they could purchase their weekly quota of opium from legalized government shops. City of Mumbai has opium dens called chandu-khanas for smoking opium. [3]

Opium had been used by emperors and the laity in the past. History has it that foreign invaders and emperors in India from the Moghul dynasty as Jahangir, Shahjehan were taking opium regularly as an entertainment. They had opium stacked away especially when they would go to their harems. Shahjehan had earmarked days as the night of merriment. Presumably he would take opium on other days as well. There are many more examples of opium eaters in the recent past.

In the present times truck drivers, laborers, sex workers and farmers have been using opium on a regular basis. Opium husk or "dodda" is sold by licensed shops on many highways in northern India. These are cheap and affordable by truck drivers who are going long distance. It helps them build stamina to work harder initially and later it becomes a routine to take it in order to start even a normal day.

In my experience I have seen seasoned opium eaters who have been taking opium all their lives and carrying on all social, financial and economic responsibilities without anyone getting to know about it. This may seem unbelievable but most opium eaters are able to do so hence it becomes difficult to estimate the number of people addicted to opium. Only the hard core opium addicts are noticeable.

Opium has been there silently for many decades in the society. There has never been an epidemic in India. Mostly the addicts came for treatment when the quality of opium dropped or when the peddlers mixed other things into it. Yet another reason has been shifting opium eaters to other strong drugs as heroin which occurred in the early eighties. This was manipulated by peddlers and pushers who would make brown sugar available and not opium and then extol the high potency and kick of brown sugar, thus talking the opium eater into trying out "smack" or brown sugar. Once the opium eater used "smack" they would buy it again and again as they had got hooked onto it. The peddler thus had been successful in creating a new smack addict.

I believe the naturally occurring drugs do not harm an individual so rapidly and drastically as does the refined or synthetic products that have come out of human laboratories. Opium, cocoa, cannabis, have all existed in many countries without having any significant destructive effect on the society. However the refined, semi-synthetic derivatives prepared by man have been many folds stronger in intoxication and damaging effects. Thus cannabis oil, heroin from opium, cocaine from cocoa have all proved to have very damaging effect on individuals, young generations and the society.

CANNABIS EPIDEMIC

There has never been a pure cannabis epidemic. Cannabis however caught the imagination and attention of the youngsters in India in the early sixties. This was largely due to the Hippie culture that had started from USA, UK and had seen many youngsters leaving their homes and getting stuck with other drug addicts in those countries.

The Beats group was a literary movement that influenced American culture and politics in the 1940s. The Beat Generation rose to prominence in America, inspiring a culture of nonconformity and social revolution. Those who were a part of the Beat Generation did not believe in straight jobs and they lived in dirty apartments selling drugs and committing crimes.

A hippie (or hippy) is a member of a counterculture, originally a youth movement that started in the United States and the United Kingdom during the mid-1960s and spread to other countries around the world. The early hippies inherited the language and countercultural values of the Beat Generation. Starting in the 1960s, Hippies created their own communities, listened to psychedelic music, embraced the sexual revolution, and used drugs such as marijuana, LSD, peyote and psilocybin mushrooms to explore altered states of consciousness.

This was also the time when Beetles the pop group had in many ways glamourized the use of drugs. They were the youth icons of those times with their hair cut in a special style called the Beatles hairstyle and their dress too was a fad with the youth. They had set up a rebellious fashion trend along with a pop culture. Beatle hairdo was accepted as being modern and fashionable in the youth in Indian metropolitan cities as well. But Indian societal value and fabric was very much intact and few college students would be seen sporting the hairstyle. In contrast today we catch up with latest fashions very fast and in a big way. Take for instance that all youngsters today sport a beard or want to sport one. Then there are those funky hairstyles which change very fast but the youngsters are not to be left behind in catching up with the trending hair styles.

Many lyrics that the beetles composed were direct lucid references to use of drugs. "Lucy in the Sky with Diamonds" refers to LSD, "Got to get you into my life" refers to Pot or Grass (Cannabis), "Happiness is a warm gun" has references as *shoot-shoot push and the pull* of addiction is nearest reference to intravenous users, "Strawberry fields forever" sung in the central park New York was a giant psychedelic leap forward (for a band that had been holding girls' hands and loving them eight days a week) has absurd lyrics and talks of *highs and lows* in the song.

Even though cannabis had been in India since ancient times as part of the ascetics, sadhus' life it had not percolated into the life of the common man in the society. There were stray and extremely rare cases of cannabis dependence in the society and a person taking cannabis was ostracized and looked down upon. However with the advent of the hippie culture the use of cannabis in university campuses became a fad. Hairstyle and bell bottomed pants had been accepted as being modern and fashionable in youth. Cannabis was very cheap therefore there was no class specificity and it had cut across all socio economic sections of society.

Youngsters from college were lured into trying out cannabis and getting stuck to it. Later many of them would get dependent on heavier drugs as LSD, Morphine, and Pethidine.

Amongst those who used cannabis only, it was carried on in later life. There was a change in the pattern of intake mainly as the cliché members had dispersed to follow their own lives, their own carriers. Many had occasional use and many had to give up.

Those who had ventured out into other drugs were the ones who would become drug addicts and the society gave them up for good.

I have felt that cannabis by itself was very less damaging and never surfaced as an open problem. The youth abused it and carried on with their day to day routine (except in cases where smoking cannabis led to psychosis). But it did open up the gates to other severely addictive and dangerous drugs as Morphine, Pethidine, LSD drugs in the sixties and seventies which took their toll on the individual and the society.

In the eighties and nineties cannabis had been a gateway to heroin or brown sugar for many individuals.

In the current times cannabis is a gateway to many new drugs as "rave party drugs", crack methamphetamines.

Cigarettes to cannabis to other drugs are the usual pattern. Alcoholics seem to be involved only in alcohol and very few would venture out to try out crack, lsd, smack. Therefore alcohol is less of a gateway drug than cannabis.

COCAINE EPIDEMIC

Cocaine had always been a very expensive drug and only the rich to super- rich people could afford it. A processed bicarbonate product called CRAX was later introduced into the market. This being much cheaper was affordable by all sections of society. Thus an epidemic of "crack" was seen in the west.

During the 1980s and 1990s, the United States was in the grips of a crack cocaine epidemic. Countless men and women saw their lives thrown into ruin as a result of this powerful, inexpensive and highly addictive form of cocaine. The streets of major cities were filled with individuals willing to sell or do anything in order to obtain their next fix. And although the mania surrounding crack would eventually die down in the late 90s, this period was unlike any other in the history of America's drug abuse history. Though crack cocaine isn't as prevalent an issue as it once was, abuse and addiction to crack cocaine are still problems in the United States.

Cocaine has always been a drug of the rich in India. However even after "crack" was introduced in India by the drug cartel there were not many users for reasons as availability of other drugs with better kick and better highs. These other drugs were cheaper as well.

We passed late 1990s to late 2000s with the fear of "crack" epidemic looking in our faces (the mental health professionals), but because of some boon there was no such phenomenon and the two decades passed in peace. This was at a time when many countries in the West were still groping for solutions to the drug (cocaine) problem.

England, Scotland, Australia, European countries France, Germany, Austria, Spain, South Africa have all been affected with the cocaine deluge.

MORPHINE AND HEROIN EPIDEMIC

Before going onto exploring the Indian heroin epidemic it would be interesting and informative to go into the history of heroin epidemics in other parts of the world.

Opium made inroads to USA in the nineteenth century when Chinese migrants came to settle down. They took up labor jobs as making of railroads, and other menial tasks to sustain their livelihood. Opium dens started mushrooming in areas as Denver, San Francisco, as well as other larger western cities. Chinese needed opium regularly and slowly the Americans too started using it. Opium was popular as a medication and recreational drug among the working class.

As medication it was used in cough, diarrhea, insomnia, and as a pain killer.

The turning point came in history of epidemic making; the moment humans used their mind to convert the natural opium into its processed derivative morphine. Morphine was discovered or rather processed by Frederic Wilhelm Adam Serturner (1783-1841), an obscure, uneducated, 21-year-old pharmacist's assistant with little equipment but loads of curiosity. This derivative proved to be a much more powerful agent at least 5 to 6 times more potent and potentially dangerous as compared to naturally occurring opium. [4]

The processing was done by boiling opium. To be more exact Morphine is extracted from opium resin or poppy straw in a series of extraction and purification steps involving water, organic solvents, and pH adjustment.

Morphine was used for only medicinal purposes. But it proved to be a double edged sword as besides its medicinal use it also proved to be highly addictive as was discovered in the subsequent years. A very large number of innocent people who had been taking morphine for cough, insomnia and pain found out that they could not do without getting their dose daily. It was beside the point whether they had their medical problem persisting or not. Once they had started morphine for curing any symptom they had to continue taking it even after the symptom was relieved. They would get severe "reaction" (withdrawal symptoms) if they missed out on the drug.

When the US Civil War came in 1860, morphine was the drug of choice to alleviate the terrible injuries of the soldiers. Doctors of the time had few tools or drugs. When a person was shot in the leg, the normal treatment was amputation. Morphine was the only thing that made the gunshot amputation and recovery tolerable. But thousands of soldiers became addicted to the drug and remained addicted after the end of the war. Addiction to morphine became known as the "Soldier's Disease."

In 1898, the Bayer pharmaceutical company began an aggressive marketing campaign to sell its commercial preparation of Heroin. That was the name they gave to their formulation of diacetylmorphine, or the product of boiling morphine for several hours. Heroin was heavily promoted as being non-addicting, and therefore an excellent treatment for opium and morphine addiction. Bronchitis, tuberculosis and other cough-inducing illnesses, chronic pain conditions were also treated with Heroin. In 1906, the American Medical Association approved Heroin for general use, and recommended that it be used in place of morphine.

This free rein soon resulted in a population of 200,000 heroin addicts in New York City. In 1914, the Harrison Narcotics Act was passed to stop abuse of cocaine, heroin and cannabis. The law made it illegal to own, use or be addicted to illicitly-obtained narcotics.

Doctors and pharmacists were required to register and pay a tax on all prescriptions. This was the beginning of arrests for drug abuse. In some areas, the majority of prisoners in federal facilities would be incarcerated there on drug charges.

With tough laws the heroin manufacturers shifted their activities to France the famous "French connection" as we know it saw the importing of unrefined heroin to Marseille, France, where it went through its final refinement before being shipped to Northeastern US cities and Europe. *Thus heroin found a new consumer market in some European countries. The abuse and addiction to heroin increased in Europe.*

The shifting of heroin manufacture later from Turkey to Southeast Asia came as a result of complicated political plays that occurred in the wake of World War II. When the dust settled, American and European crime syndicates transferred their supplier routes to the Golden Triangle - where Burma (now Myanmar), Thailand and Laos converged.

Nearly four million Americans service men and women were positioned in these areas after World War 2. In the years that followed these officers fell prey to consuming heroin. Being in a foreign land that was recovering from war ravaged scene, alcohol and drug intake were but natural choice of these stressed out service men and women. USA had a big population of service men and women who were by now dependent on heroin.

While Opium cultivation in the Golden Triangle - Thailand, Burma (Myanmar) and Laos - continued to grow. The US and France supplied Golden Triangle drug lords with ammunition, arms and air transport as a way of funding the fight against communism that was occurring in that area. This backfired once again as the soldiers got hooked onto heroin and even sold it on streets for big money.

When the servicemen returned, US had the drug addict problem of the millennium in their hands.

American soldiers have also been credited for making heroin available on the streets of Vietnam. Then in 1975, Saigon fell, cutting off the regular channels of heroin trafficking. Mexico and its poppy fields in the Sierra Madre suddenly became more important in keeping American appetites supplied.

Nixon's war on drugs soon led American agencies to begin eradicating opium fields in Mexico, using the Agent Orange that was used as a defoliant in Vietnam. This anti-drug push opened up opportunities for drug manufacturing in the Golden Crescent - Iran, Afghanistan and Pakistan. Afghanistan became the biggest supplier to Europe and the US.

In the later parts of twentieth century when enforcement to eradicate the problem did not bring results the emphasis shifted to concepts of *treatment, recovery* and still later in twenty first century to concepts of *harm reduction* wherein the treatment is directed only to reducing the intake of the intoxicant to levels where it is presumed to be less "harmful".

By 2010, a new heroin problem was making its way across the American landscape: black tar heroin. A new group of Mexican drug manufacturers and traffickers with new methods were bringing this dark-colored, sticky form of heroin to American cities, circumventing the usual heroin-trafficking routes. Overdose deaths in the cities targeted by this new group began to rise.

USA has been very vulnerable and unlucky to this day as it tops the list of Opiates and Prescription Opiates abuse in the world.

INDIAN SCENARIO OF OPIATES AND HEROIN EPIDEMIC

As drug trafficking had increased in Asia, heroin had become available in a new form. It was processed by chemical means to increase its bulk and yet retain its intoxicating effects though to a lesser degree. This was called brown sugar or "smack". Brown sugar being cheap was affordable by the middle and lower class as well.

India was initially a corridor for smuggling heroin from the golden crescent to other countries. Soon it became a dumping ground for drugs and proved to be a potentially very good market with high returns. Once the knowhow of converting heroin to brown sugar was picked up by peddlers and dealers, brown sugar was produced in many areas in India. Great damage was done. As now small to big laboratories came up in multitude, manufacturing smack in very huge quantities. These were operating from most unsuspecting areas and had hoodwinked the police for a long time.

Many such manufacturing units also came up near the licit opium farming fields where the drug lords would motivate the farmers to grow just a little extra opium plants for them in exchange of high monetary returns. These were then sent to manufacturing units where opium was extracted and processed into "brown sugar".

"Smack" had come to India in a big way during the international game event Asiad 82 hosted by INDIA, when there was a great influx of foreign tourist many of whom were already using heroin. Smack found ready customers in them especially as it was cheap.

This was also a time when a great population shift was happening. Asiad 82 saw a complete makeover of Delhi with many modern constructions coming up. New flyovers, big buildings, stadiums, hostels for players, the Asiad village a sprawling complex to accommodate the athletes from other parts of the world was built up. Many five star and four star hotels came up to accommodate tourists who would be coming to witness the games extravaganza.

People from all parts of India came to Delhi as workers, professionals, chefs, laborers, cab drivers and many more. The locals had it great with money flowing. Business saw a boom. Youngsters in many households who were already taking cigarettes or cannabis/alcohol were introduced to this dangerous and highly addictive drug. Usually the peddlers would lure youngsters by promising them a "high" never experienced before by them. Often smack was given free to hook a new comer to the drug.

Old opium addicts were talked into accepting a new drug made of opium and many times stronger. They were also told that opium quality was not the same as before and it was now costlier. The usual salesman gimmick works faster on a mind that is desperate to purchase a commodity. In this case an abuser who is going to his usual joint/peddler to purchase his quota for the day. The user reluctantly but surely switches onto a new drug that is currently very popular.

Another dark side to the opium addiction is the fact that many middle aged or young women have coaxed their paramours into consuming smack as it increases their sexual endurance. The opiates cause a much delayed ejaculation in the males. Men also who had been using it to increase sexual performance could not do without it.

Localities which had close proximity to the New Delhi railway station had cheap hotels in the past. Now there was a big mushrooming of such cheap hotels, many more new ones came up. These hotels were a popular choice of the not so rich tourist who wanted to have fun and cheap accommodation.

These tourists were usually drug dependents using multiple drugs. During the brown sugar period (early 1980s) there was increased interaction of these tourists with even the local addicts on the streets who would volunteer to get the stuff for them. This interaction had a very bad effect on the local youth who wanted to befriend foreign tourist in greed of foreign goods, drugs, companionship and a chance to get along with foreign girls. The contagion that is the drugs which exchanged many hands had actually caused infecting/addicting of all those who came along the way. Thus the brown sugar epidemic had consumed the youth and the society.

Young people from colleges, offices, hotels, guest houses, tourist agencies and many other professions and walks of life who had been experimenting with other drugs got hooked onto heroin once they tried it out.

The shanties, the slum clusters, the villages near the metropolitan cities, and the high end colonies all had peddlers from whom you could purchase your drug, and those in the high end of the social ladder would simply make a phone call to get their drugs on their doorsteps.

One staggering example of how heroin abuse has become an epidemic in Asia is India, a country that was consuming more heroin than any other country in South Asia, according to a drug report by the United Nations. Approximately 44.1 tons of heroin are produced in South Asia annually, and of that, 18.7 tons are consumed in India. As heroin abuse and addiction spreads, more and more Asians fall victim to this addiction.

The period had seen many youngsters losing their jobs, properties, families and even life. Suddenly smack addicts would show up in OPD of hospitals and private clinics in good numbers.

The government was faced with a public health problem and was not equipped at that time. The ministries came into full swing to mobilize, law, enforcement, media and health resources. Strict laws, heavy fines, new hospitals, awareness programs all came up and the problem was dealt head on. It made a big difference for the suffering addicts and it also geared us up to face any further such eventualities.

INHALANT ABUSE EPIDEMIC

There is a changing trend in substance use among children and adolescents. Substance use among children and adolescents are on the rise and causes serious concern. Amongst the various substances, tobacco and alcohol use among adolescents have been studied the most as there is an alarming increase in the incidence of tobacco and alcohol use among young people. The trend seems to be a result of many factors as failing family bonds, alcohol taking culture at home, exposure to addictive substances early in school life, stress of school, carrier, social stressors specific to the age of development and also as a means to escape boredom.

Researches into these types of addictions are funded and they are studied at all levels as social, emotional, and above all biological levels

Many of the adolescents and children are known to experiment with newer drugs. These can be cannabis in any form, cough syrups or some sleeping pills. However there is another "drug" menace which *is going unrecognized in our country.* These are the inorganic solvents or the *Inhalants* which are the easiest to procure and are available in many daily use household products. These being undetectable in the earlier days offer perfect secrecy which the addict wants. They do not want to be exposed. As they are not noticed in the earlier stages, great damage is done. The population worst affected are street children, hard core drug addicts, motor mechanics, school children, adolescents, youngsters and those working in call centers or corporate offices.

The inhalant addiction that we see represents only the tip of an iceberg. There are an enormous number of inhalant addicts who have not reported and remain undetected. This is a very serious alarm bell for everyone as damage done is to a very vulnerable population – the children and adolescents who have a long way to go and are future of the country.

The developed countries are grappling with the problem and are at their wits end as the number of such products which can be or are abused for recreational purposes and addiction is 15000 to 20000 or even more.

These include daily use items as typewriter fluids, dry cleaning fluids, paints, and thinners, many petroleum products, paraffin, nail polish removers and so on. The list is unending.

This has been the reason why no uniform laws have been formulated to cover such wide range of utility products under one umbrella. Thus any law to bring about the curbing of these chemicals has actually been ineffective.

The fact file of many countries including developed countries is very alarming. The experiences and the failure to control this epidemic benumb us.

According to the European School Project on Alcohol and Other Drugs, 20% of youth in the 12 to 16 age group have tried inhalants.

In Nairobi, Kenya, an estimated 60,000 children live on the streets and almost all are addicted to some sort of inhalant.

In the Pakistani city of Karachi there are an estimated 14,000 street kids, of whom 80% to 90% sniff glue or solvents.

About 5 percent of all deaths in teenagers in England and Wales are now caused by VSA (volatile substance abuse). The phenomenon, what was then called 'Etheromania', although essentially an urban and middle class one was considered sufficiently serious to trigger governmental reaction.

In USA 22 million adolescents have tried out inhalants and a good percentage has been taking it regularly.

Inhalant abuse was linked to 15% of deaths caused by suffocation or inhaling fluid or vomit into the lungs.

About 55% of deaths associated with inhalant abuse were caused by sudden sniffing death syndrome (SSDS), which can occur after only one use.

About 22% of inhalant abusers who died of SSDS had no history of prior inhalant use. They were first-time users.

The picture across the globe is very dismal and every country seems to affected by it.

INHALANT INCIDENCES ACROSS VARIOUS COUNTRIES

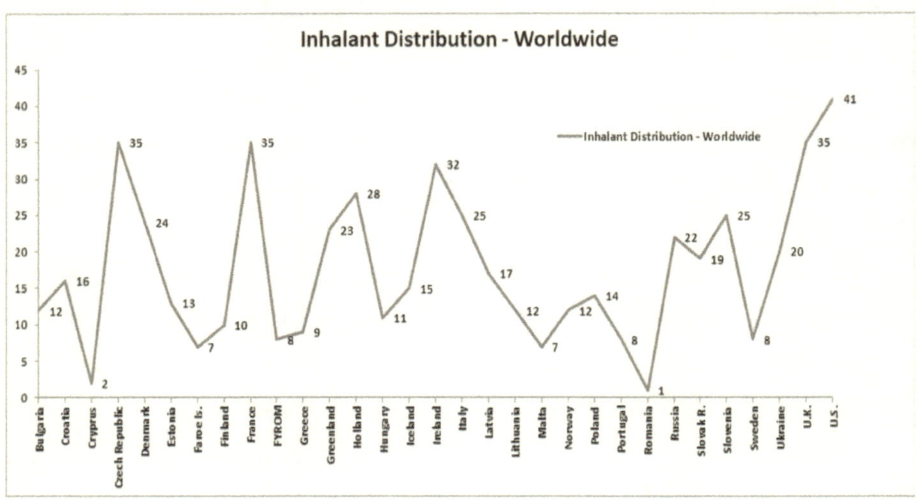

Abuse of volatile substances or inhalants has increased in children and adolescents due to its easy availability. This is increasing alarmingly in Indian cities. It has been my observation that above ninety percent of street children are consuming inhalants. A great majority of drug addicts abuse inhalants. Motor mechanics, young BPO workers, painters are known to abuse some of these products.

There are no exact figures available as the statistical analysis meets a dead end for want of exact numbers. Most of the inhalant abusers are under the blanket, hidden from everyone. The studies including the study at our center only indicates a *trend* which shows an ever increase in numbers of individuals who are accepting inhalants as a drug for intoxication.

Another trend which has been noted is the change in the type of opioids use i.e., the increase in the number of prescription drugs being abused. Poly-substance abuse is also on the rise among young people.

The epidemic of Inhalant addiction will be discussed shortly but to give the world picture refer to the graph illustrated above.

WHY DO WE CRAVE FOR DRUGS?

Humans have been fermenting alcohol for thousands of years, and generation after generation has learned to like it. The reason for this attraction probably has nothing to do with nutrition or health: "Humans love any mind-altering substance," Katharine Milton, a primatologist and human ecologist at UC Berkeley says.

The answer is straightforward. We seek intoxication for a simple reason that we are almost too scared to admit - we like it. Intoxication can be fun, sociable, memorable, therapeutic, and even mind-expanding. Saying as much in the present climate is not easy, but an increasing number of researchers now argue that unless we're prepared to look beyond the "drug problem" and acknowledge the positive aspects of intoxication, we are only seeing half the story - like researching about sex while pretending it isn't fun.

A related idea is that some people take psychoactive substances to suppress "negative pleasure". George Koob, a neuroscientist and addiction specialist at the Scripps Research Institute in La Jolla, California, has proposed that the brain has a natural system for limiting the amount of pleasure we can feel. He argues that pleasure has to be transient or humans and other animals would get so absorbed in it that they would succumb to the next predator that came along.

Koob thinks that the brain has a way of bringing us down - a kind of "anti-pleasure" mechanism. What if this system goes into overdrive? "Some people seek excessive pleasure because they are born with too much anti-pleasure," he says. "They may take drugs to feel normal."

When we are agitated or in pain, emotionally as well as physically, we seek substances that tranquillize us and sedate us and help remove these distressful feelings.

Medication with uppers and downers may be fairly easy to understand, but there are other intoxicants whose attractions are harder to fathom. These are the hallucinogens, which can't easily be explained in purely survivalist terms.

There's another drive, too, that probably plays a role in drug taking behavior. It is risk-taking. For some people taking risks is itself pleasurable. Risk taking effects different brain system to influence the pleasure circuits.

Taking intoxicants is a naturally occurring phenomenon in the animal kingdom

During the Vietnam War, Siegel and his team filmed water buffalo grazing on opium poppies to the point of addiction.

And animals don't just take downers: there are numerous reports of goats guzzling stimulants such as coffee beans and the herbal amphetamine khat.

The drive to medicate mood is pervasive throughout the animal kingdom, Siegel says, and he and his colleagues have documented thousands of examples.

Elephants, for instance, enjoy the taste of fermented fruit. They will usually just browse it, but if they lose their mate (elephants usually have single mate for life) they may seek oblivion in an alcoholic fruit binge, even drinking neat ethanol if researchers provide it. It's hard not to conclude that, like humans, they are drowning their sorrows.

When tired or depressed, we too seek stimulants. According to some researchers, including Grob, this medicinal use is an underlying thread running through all forms of intoxication.

Siegel believes there is a strong biological drive to seek intoxication. "It's the fourth drive," he says. "After hunger, thirst and sex, there is intoxication." Whether we are seeking pleasure, stimulation, pain relief or escape, at the root of this drive, he says, is the motivation to feel "different from normal" - what has sometimes been called "a holiday from reality".

As Weil pointed out in his 1973 book The Natural Mind, from an early age children experiment with spinning around or hyperventilating to experience mind-altering giddiness.

NEUROTRANSMITTERS AND ADDICTION

How do drugs work in the brain?

Drugs are chemicals that affect the brain by tapping into its communication system and interfering with the way neurons normally send, receive, and process information. Some drugs, such as marijuana and heroin, can activate neurons because their chemical structure mimics that of a natural neurotransmitter. This similarity in structure "fools" receptors and allows the drugs to attach onto and activate the neurons. Although these drugs mimic the brain's own chemicals, they don't activate neurons in the same way as a natural neurotransmitter, and they lead to abnormal messages being transmitted through the network.

Other drugs, such as amphetamine or cocaine, can cause the neurons to release abnormally large amounts of natural neurotransmitters or prevent the normal recycling of these brain chemicals. This disruption produces a greatly amplified and distorted message, thus ultimately disrupting communication channels.

How do drugs work in the brain to produce pleasure?

Most drugs of abuse directly or indirectly target the brain's reward system by flooding the circuit with dopamine. Dopamine is a neurotransmitter that is present in regions of the brain which regulate movement, emotion, motivation, and *feelings of pleasure*. When activated at normal levels, this system rewards our natural behaviors. Over stimulating the system with drugs, however, produces euphoric effects, which strongly reinforce the behavior of drug use, teaching the user to repeat it.

The Dopamine neurotransmitter system is responsible for pleasures that we experience in our daily living right from pleasure we experience with good food to sex, music, exercise, sports, gambling and all others. Dopamine system is responsible for reward, euphoria and motivation besides the other functions as seen in the illustration below.

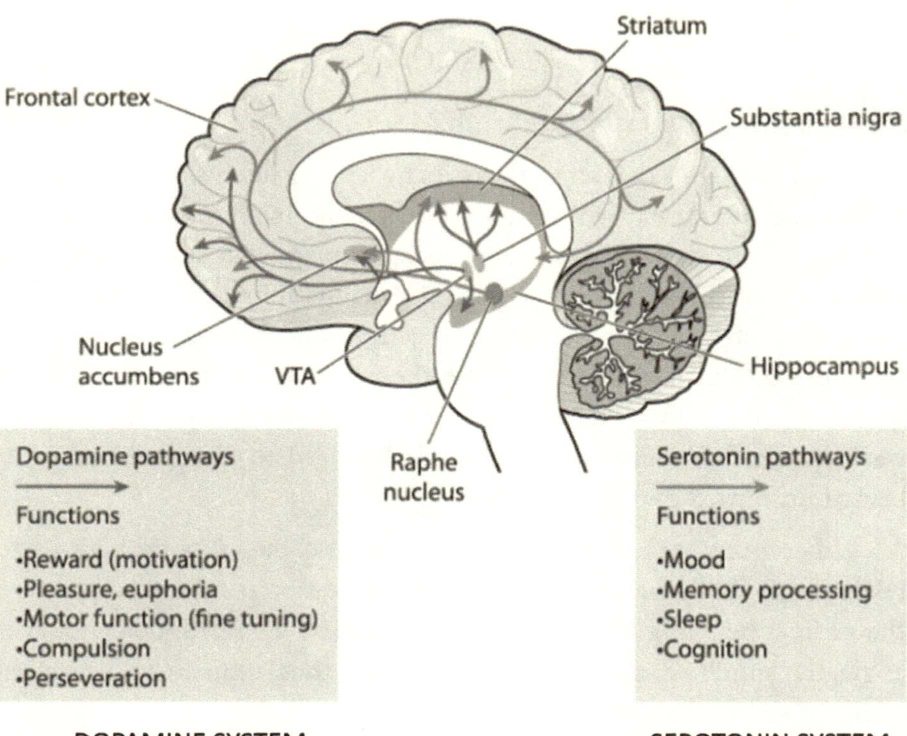

In the illustration given below one can see the immense and abnormal release of Dopamine under the influence of Cocaine as compared to a normal release after food intake. The release in normal circumstances as in eating food, sense of success, reward is conducive to normal living and normal emotions.

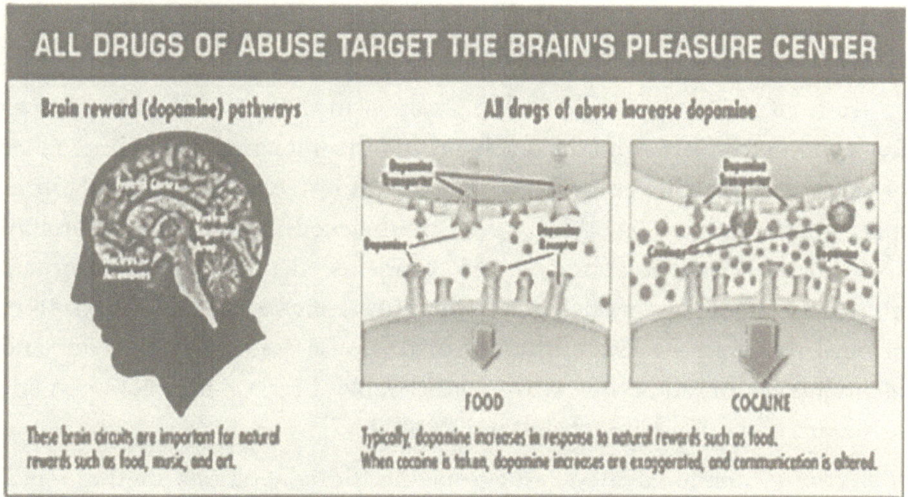

SEROTONIN SYSTEM

Another neurotransmitter system is the Serotonin system .The majority of the body's serotonin, between 80-90%, can be found in the gastrointestinal tract. Serotonin that is used inside the brain must be produced within it. It is thought that serotonin can *affect mood and social behavior*, appetite and digestion, sleep, memory and sexual desire and function.

Functions of Serotonin

As a neurotransmitter, serotonin influences both directly and indirectly the majority of brain cells. The following is a list of functions that serotonin could affect:

Mood: It is most well-known for its role in the brain where it plays a major part in mood, anxiety and happiness. Illicit mood-altering drugs such *as Ecstasy and LSD* cause a massive rise in serotonin levels.

The use of psychoactive drugs is a wide spread behavior in human societies. The systematic use of a drug requires the establishment of different (drug use-associated) behaviors which need to be learned and controlled, like arranging finance, procuring a drug, using the technique specific to the drug. However, controlled drug use may eventually develop into compulsive drug use and addiction, a major psychiatric disorder with severe consequences for the individual and society.

Role of the serotonergic (5-HT) system in the establishment of *drug use-associated behaviors* on the one hand and the transition and maintenance of addiction on the other hand for the drugs: cocaine, amphetamine, methamphetamine, MDMA (3,4 **methylenedioxymethamphetamine**) also called ecstasy, morphine/heroin, cannabis, alcohol, and nicotine are irrefutable. There is a crucial, but distinct involvement of the 5-HT system in both processes i.e. establishment of drug-use associated behavior and mantainence of addiction with considerable overlap between psycho-stimulant and opioidergic drugs and alcohol.

A new functional model suggests specific adaptations in the 5-HT system, which coincides with the establishment of controlled drug use-associated behaviors. These serotonergic adaptations render the nervous system susceptible to the transition to compulsive drug use behaviors and often overlap with genetic risk factors for addiction. Serotonergic neuro-adaptations induced by first drug exposure pave the way for the establishment of addiction. [5]

Other functions of the serotonin system are:

Bowel function: Most of the body's serotonin is found in the gastrointestinal tract where it regulates bowel function and movements. It also plays a part in reducing the appetite while consuming a meal.

Clotting: Its third major role is in the formation of blood clots. Serotonin is released by platelets when there is a wound, and the resulting vasoconstriction (narrowing of the tiny arteries - arterioles) reduces blood flow and aids the formation of blood clots.

Nausea- If you eat something that is toxic or irritating, more serotonin is produced in the gut to increase transit time and expel the irritant in diarrhea. This increase in blood serotonin levels also causes nausea by stimulating the nausea area in the brain.

The table below gives the neurotransmitter systems that are involved in various drugs of abuse. It also highlights the effect the drugs produce after binding with the neurotransmitter system.

Drug	Neurotransmitter	Drug target	Effect after binding
Opiates (morphine, heroin)	Endorphins	μ and δ opioid (agonist)	Activate Gi/Go Activate K+ channels
Psycho-stimulants (cocaine, amphetamines)	Dopamine (DA)	Dopamine transporter (DAT) (antagonist)	Increase synaptic DA; stimulate presynaptic and postsynaptic DA receptors
Nicotine	Acetylcholine	Nicotinic acetylcholine receptors (nAChRs) (agonist)	Stimulates cation channel (may desensitize)
Alcohol	γ-Aminobutyric acid (GABA) Glutamate	$GABA_A$ receptor (agonist)	Activate Cl− channel
Marijuana (Δ9-tetrahydrocannabinol)	Anandamide	Cannabinoid CB_1 (agonist)	Activate Gi/Go
Hallucinogens (Phencyclidine, ketamine)		NMDA receptor channel (antagonist)	Inhibit Ca2+ entry

GENETIC STUDIES

FosB – (FBJ murine osteosarcoma viral oncogene homolog B), also known as FOSB is a protein that, in humans, is encoded by the FOSB gene. Gene expression is the process by which information from a gene is used in the synthesis of a functional gene product. These products are proteins, but they can also be functional RNA.

ΔFOSB or Delta FOSB is a truncated splice variant of FOSB protein. *ΔFOSB has been implicated as a critical factor in the development of virtually all forms of behavioral and drug addictions.* In the brains reward system, it is linked to changes in a number of other gene products, such as CREB (CREB i.e. cyclic AMP response element-binding) and Sirtuins.

CREB influences circadian rhythm, corticotrophin releasing factor, somatostatins, tyrosine and many more including long term memory.

Sirtuins have been implicated in influencing a wide range of cellular processes like aging, transcription, apoptosis (natural death of cells in the normal process of growth), inflammation and stress resistance, as well as energy efficiency and alertness during low-calorie situations. Sirtuins can also control circadian clocks and mitochondrial biogenesis.

In the body, ΔFOSB regulates the destination of mesenchyme precursor cells to the adipocyte (fat forming cells) or osteoblast lineage (brings about formation of bones)

In the nucleus Accumbens, ΔFOSB functions as a "sustained molecular switch" and "master control protein" in the development of an addiction. In other words, once "turned on" (sufficiently overexpressed) ΔFOSB triggers a series of transcription events (gene inscriptions for events) that ultimately produce an addictive state (i.e., compulsive reward-seeking involving a particular stimulus). This state is sustained for months after cessation of drug use due to the abnormal and exceptionally long half-life of ΔFOSB isoforms. The *nucleus Accumbens is a brain structure that is part of our pleasure and reward system.*

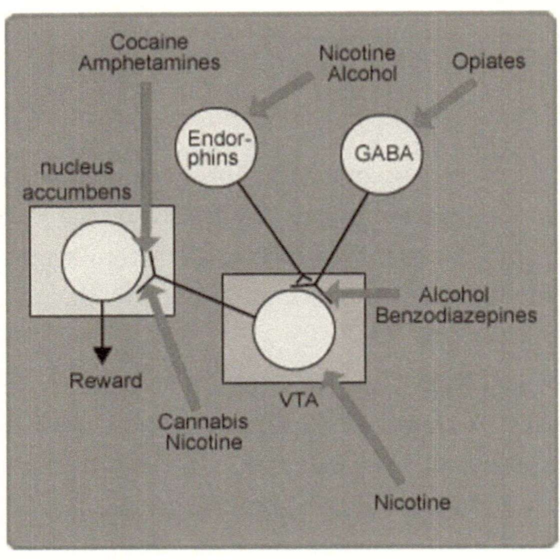

Addiction pathways. VTA – Ventral Tegmental Area, Nucleus Accumbens

ΔFOSB expression in D1-type nucleus Accumbens neurons directly and positively regulates drug self-administration and reward sensitization through positive reinforcement while decreasing sensitivity to aversion. Based upon the accumulated evidence, a medical review from late 2014 argued that Accumbal ΔFOSB expression can be used as an *addiction biomarker* and that the degree of Accumbal ΔFOSB induction by a drug is a measure for how addictive it is relative to other drugs.

Delta-FOSB also builds up in *"natural addictions,"* such as high consumption of fatty/sugary foods, and high levels of aerobic exercise and sexual activity (and no doubt, porn addiction). Some sources suggest that it declines around the 6-8th week of abstinence. We suspect this decline in Delta FOSB is behind the big improvements people see once they get to the 8 week mark. [6]

INHALANTS

WHAT ARE INHALANTS?

Inhalants are volatile substances that produce chemical vapors that can be inhaled to induce a psychoactive, or mind-altering, effect. Although other abused substances can be inhaled, the term "inhalants" is used to describe a variety of substances whose main common characteristic is that they are rarely, if ever, taken by any route other than inhalation. This definition encompasses a broad range of chemicals that may have different pharmacological effects and are found in hundreds of different products.

Inhalants include a broad range of household and industrial chemicals that have come up tragically as intoxicants in a *manner not intended by the manufacturer*. They are inhaled at room temperature through volatilization (in the case of gasoline or acetone) or from a pressurized container (e.g., nitrous oxide or butane), *and do not include drugs that are sniffed after burning or heating*. For example, amyl nitrite (poppers), nitrous oxide and toluene – the solvent used in contact cement and model airplane glue – are considered inhalants, but smoking tobacco, cannabis, and crack are not, even though these drugs are inhaled (as smoke).

CLASSIFICATION OF INHALANTS

There are hundreds of thousands of household and industrial products which can be volatilized readily and are subject to abuse. Inhalant abuse research has been hampered by a lack of consensus on whether or not there are sub-classifications of abused inhalants as based on *chemical structure, form or intended use of the product or* pharmacological *properties*.

As there is not a sufficient database on unique chemicals, their pharmacological properties and their patterns of abuse, we have to use caution developing sub classifications of inhalants which are not based on strong scientific evidence. This is particularly true for classifications that might have a tendency to create enduring groupings that are shown subsequently to be premature or that may apply only to one country or cultural group.

Attempts to categorize them would mean many loose and controversial points.

There are several basis on which abused inhalants have been classified in various publications and by individual investigators. Thus classifications have been based on:-

1.   *Chemical,* structure.

2.   *Form,* such as gas, vapor, aerosol or liquid.

3.   *Product type,* such as fuels, anesthetics, cleaners, glues, aerosol products, etc.

4.   *Pharmacological properties.*

As we already know there are more than 15000 chemicals which have domestic and industrial use and are commonly available. Many of these are used as inhalants for intoxication.

One classification system lists four general categories of inhalants —

- *Volatile solvents*

- *Aerosols*

- *Gases*

- *Nitrites*

Based on the forms in which they are often found in household, industrial, and medical products.

<u>Volatile solvents</u> are liquids that vaporize at room temperature. They are found in a multitude of inexpensive, easily available products used for common household and industrial purposes. These include paint thinners

and removers, dry-cleaning fluids, degreasers, gasoline, glues, correction fluids, and felt-tip markers.

<u>Aerosols</u> are sprays that contain propellants and solvents. They include spray paints, deodorant and hair sprays, vegetable oil sprays for cooking, and fabric protector sprays.

<u>Gases</u> include medical anesthetics as well as gases used in household or commercial products. Medical anesthetics include ether, chloroform, halothane, and nitrous oxide (commonly called "laughing gas"). Nitrous oxide is the most abused of these gases and can be found in whipped cream dispensers and products that boost octane levels in racing cars. Other household or commercial products containing gases include butane lighters, propane tanks, and refrigerants.

<u>Nitrites</u> often are considered a special class of inhalants. Unlike most other inhalants, which act directly on the central nervous system (CNS), nitrites act primarily to dilate blood vessels and relax the muscles. While other inhalants are used to alter mood, nitrites are used primarily as sexual enhancers. Nitrites include cyclohexyl nitrite, isoamyl (amyl) nitrite, and isobutyl (butyl) nitrite and are commonly known as "poppers" or "snappers." Amyl nitrite is used in certain diagnostic procedures and was prescribed in the past to treat some patients for heart pain. Nitrites now are prohibited by the Consumer Product Safety Commission but can still be found, sold in small bottles labeled as "video head cleaner," "room odorizer," "leather cleaner," or "liquid aroma."

I have attempted to classify them in a table framework that addresses classification based on –

- Chemical structure

- Form of the substance

- There is an additional column which has great importance as it shows ways of consuming. One would get a ready reference and not waste time flipping pages. I felt this would be a convenient illustration with most information on a single page.

I would detail the ways in which inhalants are consumed in the subsequent chapters.

Classification of Inhalants

DRUGS	CHEMICAL COMPOSITION	MODE OF TAKING
Adhesives • "TUCKT" tube for tyre punctures of bicycles • "OK" tube for tyre punctures of cars	• Chlorinated solvents • Toluene, acetone • Methyl ethyl chloride • Methyl chloride	• Inhaling • Huffing
Solvents • Paint removers	• Toluene, methylene chloride, methanol, acetone	• Inhaling (by placing the fluid on a piece of cloth, in a tin box with cotton)
• Nail polish removers	• Acetone, toluene, ethyl acetate	• Sniffing (iquid put on a cloth and sniffed at regular intervals)
• Paint thinners, lacquers • Dry-cleaning fluids	• Acetone, petroleum distillates • Tetra chloro ethylene, tri chloroethylene, xylene, petroleum distillates, hydrocarbon	
• Stain removers		

DRUGS	CHEMICAL COMPOSITION	MODE OF TAKING
Fuels • Leaded • Unleaded	• Hexane, septane, octane, etc. +BTX or olefins, cyclic aromatic HC	• Inhaled after placing in a box or on a piece of cloth
Correction fluids • Type-writer fluids	• Toluene	• Sniffed • Inhaled
Lighter propellant • Aerosols spray	• Butane, propane	• They are sprayed on a cloth and then sniffed and inhaled
• Deodorants • PC cleaners	• Butane, iso-propane • Dimethyl ether, HFC	
Lubricants • Grease	• Petroleum distillates	• Placed on a roti or bread and hot dal spread on it. The fumes are inhaled and the bread eaten.

DRUGS	CHEMICAL COMPOSITION	MODE OF TAKING
• Pain balms	• Gandepura oil (wintergreen oil), nilgiri oil, pudina flower, laung oil, turpentine oil	• Spread on bread, placed in a freezer then eaten
• Vaseline	• Paraffin in alcohol base	• Sniffed and inhaled
• Camphor	• Camphor and carbon disulphide	• Fumes are inhaled. Chewed
• Crackers		• Chewing
• Karborized match-sticks	• Red phosphorus	• Fumes are inhaled
• Lime	• Calcium hydroxide	• Rubbed in palms and inhaled

DRUGS	CHEMICAL COMPOSITION	MODE OF TAKING
*Miscellaneous		
• Phenyl	• Coal tar oil, coal tar acid, phenolic acid	• Inhaled, sniffed on cloth or directly from the bottle
• Antiseptic liquid	• Chloroxylenol terminel, BP absolute alcohol (denatured)	• Inhaled from cloth placed between palms
• Naphthalene balls	• Naphthalene, paradichlorobenzene	• Inhaled through a cloth or rubbed between the palms and inhaled • Licked at regular intervals
• Exhaust fumes	• Carbon monoxide, unburnt hydrocarbons, sulphur	• Inhaled while the engine is on
• Burning rubber and tyres	• Unburnt HC - methane, ethane, butane, SO_2	• Inhaled by sitting around it

INHALANT ABUSERS

CHARACTERISTICS OF A PERSON ABUSING INHALANTS

The individuals who have been using alcohol/drugs for some time develop specific characteristics. These are peculiarly associated with the drug of abuse. The presentation, behavior, attitude all stand out in each addiction as a brand mark. Thus alcoholics are different (in appearance) from heroin addicts and also cannabis abuser. Inhalant abusers also over long term abuse eventually evolve into individuals with specific characteristics. The following are salient features of inhalant abusers.

- Delinquency
- Theft and burglary
- Poor school attendance
- Frequent suspension and expulsion from school
- Social outcast
- Lack of parental control or guidance
- Attention deficit
- Poor academic performance
- Low intelligence quotient
- Antisocial personality and behavior
- Depressive disorders —the patient remains withdrawn and sulks away from people.
- Emotional problems (specifically anxiety, depression, and anger)
- Impulsivity

- Low self-esteem
- Peer pressure with drug influence
- Memory impairment
- Poor health
- Sick appearance
- Stains around the mouth and nose.

CATEGORIES OF INHALANT ABUSERS

Dr Neil Rosenberg and Dr Sharp have identified and broadly classified inhalant abusers into four categories. These are-

- Transient Social User- Short history of use with friends
- Chronic Social User-long history of use more than 5 years, daily use with friends, embroiled in legal issues, brain damage, poor social skill.
- Transient Isolate user –Short history of use, Solo use.
- Chronic Isolate User-Long history of use more than 5 years, solo use, involved in legal issues, poor skills, brain damage. [7]

REASONS FOR USING INHALANTS

Why the inhalants have caught the fantasy of youngsters? The reasons are mentioned below.

- Easy to obtain
- Easy to use
- Immediate High
- Very Cheap
- Comes in convenient packages which can be carried on person without being detected.
- The high wears off fast thus short enjoyments also possible.
- Legal to carry and purchase.
- Undetected in low doses.

WAYS OF CONSUMING

Inhalants are volatile substances that produce chemical vapors that can be inhaled to induce a psychoactive, or mind-altering, effect. Although other abused substances can be inhaled, the term "inhalants" is used to describe a variety of substances whose main common characteristic is that they are rarely, if ever, taken by any route other than inhalation.

Generally, inhalant abusers will abuse any available substance. This substitution and a desperate need for a 'high' compel an inhalant abuser to try out anything that lets out fumes/vapors. Examples of inhaling burning match stick smoke, burning plastic/vehicular rubber tyres smoke are common amongst poor addicts. However effects produced by individual inhalants vary and some users will go out of their way to obtain their favorite inhalant or give up the inhalant that does not bring the desired effect.

How are Inhalants Used?

Inhalants can be breathed in through the nose or the mouth in a variety of ways, such as—

"SNIFFING": "Sniffing" or "snorting" fumes from containers. This is also done by applying the fluid to a piece of cloth and taking relaxed or deep sniffs to deliver the inhalant into the lungs and get a high.

"HUFFING": In this case the inhalant is put on a piece of cloth and vapors inhaled through an open mouth an act very similar to when smoking a "hookah".

"PUFFING": The substance to be inhaled is applied to the palm and rubbed thus generating vapors. The vapors are then inhaled through the mouth from one end of the closed fist.

"BAGGING": In this case the inhalant is placed inside a plastic bag and shook vigorously thus filling the bag with good amount of vapors. The vapor is then inhaled deeply through the nose making sure not to waste it by holding it air tight around the nose-mouth.

"PARTYING":   Usually when there are a number of inhalant abusers they would make a born- fire of inhalants and gather around it to inhale the fumes.

"SPRAYING":   Aerosols are directly sprayed into the nose or mouth and inhaled.

"INHALING":   Balloons are filled with nitrous oxide gas and inhaled at regular intervals.

INHALING automobile fumes by hanging behind vehicles which have their engines running. This way they get to inhale the exhaust fumes which give a high.

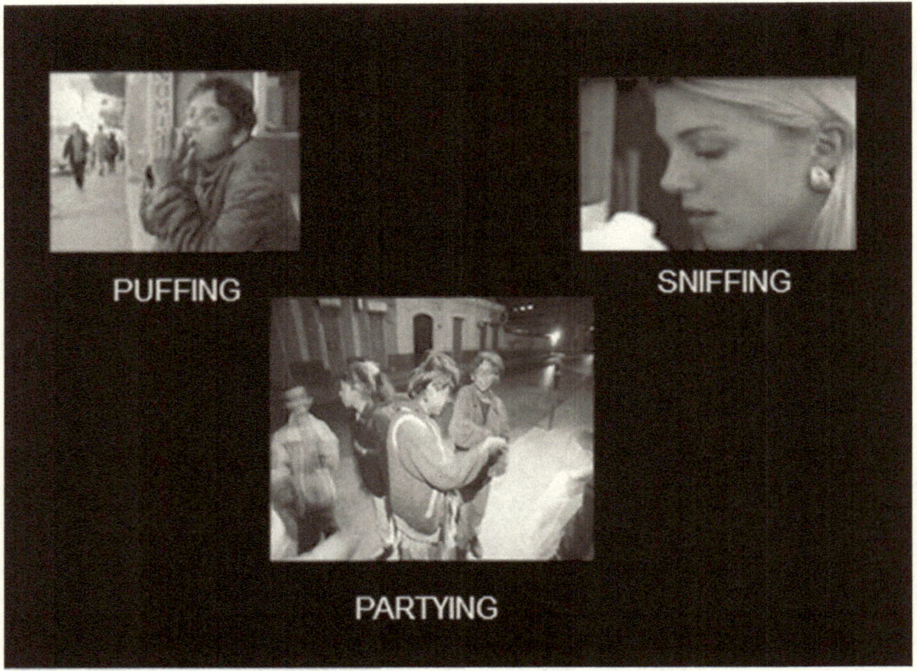

Some other known ways of consuming inhalants beats your imagination. These are not unknown.

"EATING":   Putting glue on breads and eating it. It is still an Inhalant even though the abuser is using it differently to get a "kick". The high is in eating. Some effect that is likely to take place after it has been metabolized by the liver. Seems less likely that the effect would be the same when inhaled.

Spreading Iodex a rubifacient on bread then placing it in a refrigerator to eat it later maybe after an hour or two.

Pouring drops of Amrutanjan a rubifacient in tea and drinking it.

"LICKING":   Licking naphthalene balls to get a high.

"CHEWING":   Chewing camphor, sometimes crackers.

These are examples which do not have any scientific explanation to prove how one could get a high with these. But I believe they are just past times which have caught onto a person's obsessive desire to try new means to get a high.

These are also examples which redefine "Inhalants" as agents which are not necessarily inhaled. This is contrary to the universally accepted definition. However these abusers are miniscule and are exception rather than the rule.

PATHOPHYSIOLOGY

Inhalants are highly lipid soluble; they easily cross both alveolar membranes in the lungs and the blood-brain barrier to reach high concentrations in the brain. Inhalation avoids first-pass hepatic metabolism so the onset is fast. Symptom at onset is noted within seconds, and peak plasma concentration occurs 15–30 minutes after inhalation. The inhaled concentration depends on the mode of administration. Sniffing offers the lowest concentration, followed by huffing, and bagging which offers the highest concentration.

At low doses of ambient toluene around 200 ppm(parts per million) there is headache, sluggishness, slow reflexes and weakness.

Confusion, dullness, loss of self-control, ringing in the head, blurred vision develops in those exposed to 600 ppm.

Euphoria, slurred speech, in co-ordination, depressed reflexes and nystagmus develops when levels reach 800 ppm

The majority of acute behavioral effects appear to be due to changes in receptor and/or ion channel activity in the brain in the presence of inhalants. The GABA, glycine and Serotonin receptors show activation. The NMDA (excitatory) receptor shows an inhibition of activity. There are also nonspecific interactions of neurotransmitter systems when high concentrations of inhalants are abused.

But abusers continue with taking further dose to sustain the euphoria and the toluene levels reach dangerous levels giving rise to acute encephalopathy, delirium.

METABOLISM

Toluene an active chemical in many inhalants has been studied more in detail and the metabolism of toluene is discussed here. Brief mention of other chemicals in inhalants and their metabolism is discussed with each inhalant.

After exposure the inhalant (toluene) is absorbed through the lungs and goes into the blood stream to be distributed throughout the body. Most inhaled Toluene is metabolized in the liver by conversion to Benzoic acid by enzymes Alcohol dehydrogenase and Aldehyde dehydrogenase.

Benzoic acid is then conjugated with Glycine to form Hippuric acid (80 %) OR it combines with Glucronic acid to form Benzyl glucronide (20 %). Both these metabolites are highly water soluble and are readily eliminated through the kidneys.

Hippuric acid is the main metabolite and 75 % of the inhaled toluene is eliminated through the kidneys within first 12 hours of exposure. Toluene is retained longer in the adipose tissues where its ½ life is 0.5 to 3 days. Toluene is highly lipophilic (affinity for fatty tissues) which explains its rapid concentration in the lipid rich central nervous system. The high concentration of toluene in the central nervous system also gives rise to the toxic effects.

With a few exceptions, *elimination occurs primarily through the lungs*, with many inhaled compounds eliminated unchanged by exhalation. Some of the inhalants, including alkyl nitrites, aromatics, and methylene chloride, undergo significant hepatic metabolism that can produce damaging free nitrites and toxic carbon monoxide as byproducts which is toxic to liver.

INHALANTS – MODE OF ACTION

Ethylene glycol or sweet alcohol is the simplest member of the glycol family of organic compounds. A glycol is an alcohol with two hydroxyl groups on adjacent carbon atoms (a 1,2-diol). It is an important constituent **of** *Coolants, Antifreeze Solvents, and Explosive, Anti-corrosive-* behaves as Ethanol .Ethylene Glycol metabolized by alcohol dehydrogenase. Ethylene Glycol is *more* potent than alcohol hence the "high" is faster and more severe.

Isopropyl alcohol and acetone-Component *of After Shave Lotion, Window Cleaners, Nail Polish Removers* is rapidly absorbed from the lungs and stomach and behaves like Ethanol causing intoxication

Methanol-Component of *Shellacs, Varnishes, Paint Removers, Copy Machine Fluid* acts as ethanol and produces similar effects and intoxication.

Other *Alcohols* used are n-propyl alcohol, butyl alcohol, secondary butyl, diethylene glycol, tri-ethylene alcohol, and glycerol-all have abuse potential and prevalence. These are used in perfumes and solvents.

As we have detailed earlier Alcohol exerts its effect by binding onto Inhibitory neurotransmitter system of GABA gamma amino butyric acid and Glycine neurotransmitter system thus bringing about its inhibitory influence.

On the other hand it acts on the excitatory neurotransmitter system as the Glutamate neurotransmitter system, the Aspartate, and the Adenosine system. It has an inhibitory effect on this system.

Short-term alcohol exposure tilts this balance in favor of inhibitory influences. After long-term alcohol exposure, however, the brain attempts to compensate by tilting the balance back toward equilibrium. These neurological changes occur as the development of tolerance to alcohol's effects. When alcohol consumption is abruptly discontinued or reduced, these compensatory changes are no longer opposed as alcohol is not present, thereby leading to the excitation of neurotransmitter systems and the development of alcohol withdrawal syndrome.

Aromatic Hydrocarbons

Toluene, Benzene, Xylene – These acts as Central Nervous System depressants resulting in anesthesia, intoxication. Toluene a recent study showed *activates the brains dopamine system thus giving a sense of reward and acts as a reinforcement to continue the act (adhesives, paint removers)*

Chlorinated Hydrocarbons

Tetrachloroethylene, trichloroethylene-used in dry cleaning industry-*affects CNS as a depressant.* Thus having effects as headache, dizziness, numbness of hands, apprehension, and partial paralysis of extremities, loss of equilibrium, coma, and Sleep apnea syndrome. In higher dosage it results in death.

Methylene chloride-used in paint removers, dye industries, and degreasers emits fumes which are highly toxic. These *are metabolized to Carbon monoxide in the body.* Intoxication effects are lightheadedness, drunken feeling, ataxia, confusion. Higher dose is lethal.

Aliphatic Hydrocarbons

Also called petroleum distillates these are n-hexane-heptane and are used as a solvent in paints and thinners. They have a narcotic and sedating effect in addition to causing peripheral neuropathy *and paralysis of limbs which remain permanent on long exposure.*

Benzene, mineral spirits and kerosene are other substances in this group

Esters-ethyl acetate.

Glycols-ethylene glycols.

Methyl ethyl ketone, acetone.

Carbon Monoxide

The intoxication is by inhaling automobile exhaust fumes, inhaling fumes from paraffin stove burning, fumes of generators, industrial processes.

John Burdon Sanderson Haldane FRS was an English scientist known for his work in the study of physiology, genetics, evolutionary biology, and in mathematics.

Haldane's experiment on himself by inhaling carbon monoxide gas demonstrated the following data of effects of carbon monoxide on the human being:-

0.01% of carbon monoxide in the atmosphere =10% of carboxy-hemoglobin in blood this gives no appreciable symptoms.

0.02%-0.025%-causes distinct toxic symptoms relished as a high.

This is =20%-30% of carboxy-hemoglobin in blood enough to cause hypoxia leading to confusion, clumsiness, emotional lability, hallucinations, impaired judgment.

Higher concentration exceeding 50% carboxy-hemoglobin leads to death

The modes of action are thought to result from the ability of carbon monoxide to bind to heme and alter function and/or metabolism of heme proteins in blood. Formation of carboxyhemoglobin(CO Hb) decreases the O2 carrying capacity of blood and impairs release of O2 from Hemoglobin for its utilization in tissues and brain.

Oil of Westergreen

Popular pain reliever ointments contain salicylates, and are used as a rubeficiant. One teaspoonful of wintergreen oil contains 7 gram of salicylate=22 adult Aspirin tablets. Iodex, Amrutanjan Cream preparations vary in salicylate concentration and effect multi-organ system. Effect on CNS- Vertigo, tinnitus, disorientation, seizures, lethargy.

Respiratory system- stimulates respiration, causing respiratory alkalosis.

Salicylates in dosing of 150 mg/kg of body weight results in mild toxicity with symptoms of nausea vomiting and dizziness. In moderate to high dosing of 150-300 mg/kg the toxicity is very high with confusion, headache, muscle twitching, and hyperventilation. At severely high dosing of (300–500 mg/kg) delirium sets in along with seizures, coma, and respiratory arrest and death.

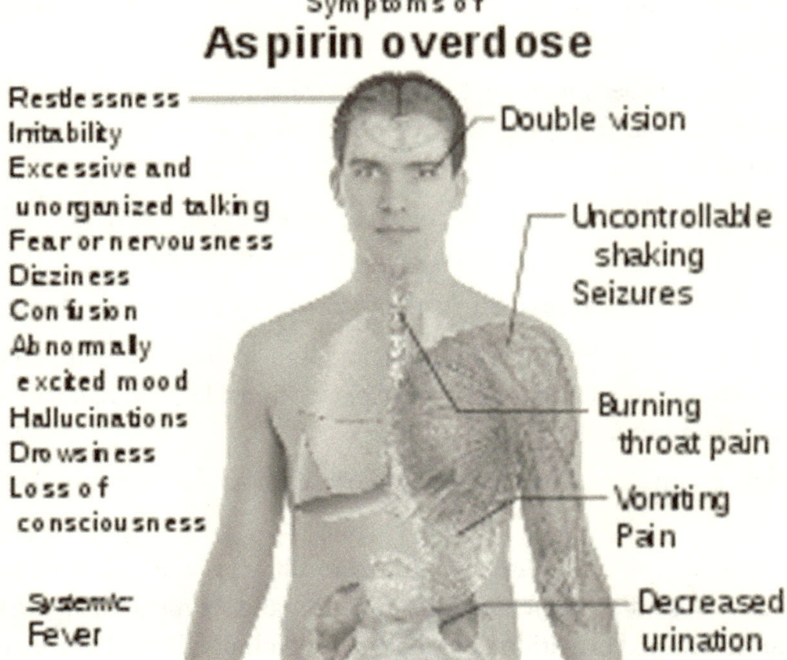

Camphor

Camphor used to be made by distilling the bark and wood of the camphor tree. Today, camphor is chemically manufactured from turpentine oil. It is used in products such as Vicks Vaporub which is a popular cream used as a local painkiller by superficial application.

Effects of Camphor

Central Nervous System-mild intoxication leads to mild excitation, higher exposure leads to Grand mal seizures, status epilepticus. Gastric –On ingestion leads to a feeling of warmth. Sore throat, dilated pupils, psychic symptoms similar to alcohol intoxication.

Phenyl

Phenyl group- The phenyl group or phenyl ring is a cyclic group of atoms with the formula C6H5. Phenyl groups are closely related to benzene and can be viewed as a benzene ring, minus a hydrogen atom, which may be replaced by some other element or compound to serve as a functional group. Acts as a CNS depressant causing confusion, light headedness, incoordination.

Naphthalene Balls

NAPTHALENE & PARADICHLOROBENZENE- Ingredients act as CNS depressant in much the same way as Methyl butyl ketone, Acetone leading to ataxia, confusion, light headedness, slurred speech.

Para dichlorobenzene is less toxic. On chronic use- causes liver and kidney damage.

Naphthalene-acutely toxic resulting in rapid cirrhosis, renal failure, hemolysis and seizures.

Carbon Disulphide

Used as a solvent in making camphor.

Mode of action-Forms Dithiocarbamates which acts on the Central Nervous System to produce intoxication. It is a very toxic and a neurotoxic compound.

Disturbs Vitamin metabolism-B6 and nicotinic acid.

Impairs Catecholamine metabolism. Catechol amines cause general physiological changes that prepare the body for physical activity (fight-or-flight response). Some typical effects are increases in heart rate, blood pressure, blood glucose levels, and a general reaction of the sympathetic nervous system. The dynamic equilibrium of these functions is jeopardized.

Dopamine beta hydroxylase enzyme is inhibited-Dopamine not converted to norepinephrine, thus increase in Dopamine and decrease in Norepinephrine levels at the synaptic level.

Disturbs Lipid metabolism.

Many inhalant abusers suffer from at least one co-occurring psychological disorder; a pre-existing serotonin or other brain chemical imbalance may have motivated the initial bout of inhalant abuse.

EFFECT OF INHALANTS ON THE HUMANS

MEDICAL EFFECTS

Pathological Aspects

The Toluene, Benzene and other ingredients in the hydrocarbons are very toxic to the body organs and their effects reflect very rapidly in the individual abusing inhalants. The effect on the various organ systems affected is detailed below.

Brain

Most of the damage inflicted by inhalant abuse initially affects the brain. Tremors and uncontrollable shaking are observed in those who abuse inhalants for a long period.

Inhalants also affect eyesight, causing double vision and other sight disorders.

Many who abuse inhalants experience seizures. Headaches are common.

Damage to the brain may lead to changes in personality.

Memory loss, decreased cognitive functioning, slurred speech impair social functioning greatly.

The Magnetic Resonance Imaging of the inhalant abusers brain shows abnormalities which are characteristically seen in organic brain damage associated with dementia.

Those who abuse toluene may have significantly wider cerebellar and cerebral sulci and larger ventricular systems. Damage to the myelin sheath and altered size/shape of the corpus callosum may ensue with inhalant use.

There is also a marked atrophy in the brain size of inhalant abusers.

Toluene Leuko Encephalopathy is a severe toxic effect of Toluene on White matter of the brain. It has become a prototypal example of White matter Dementia and underscores the significance of cerebral white matter in neuro-behavioral functions.

Neuropathological examination shows cerebral and cerebellar MYELIN loss, Axonal loss and Perivascular macrophages. The myelin loss is pronounced in the corpus callosum area. There is loss of differentiation between gray and white matter throughout the Central Nervous System.

The degree of loss is variable depending on age of onset of abuse, dose, co-existent abuse of other drugs and genetic predisposition (polymorphism in the gene encoding the enzyme Aldehyde Dehydrogenase)

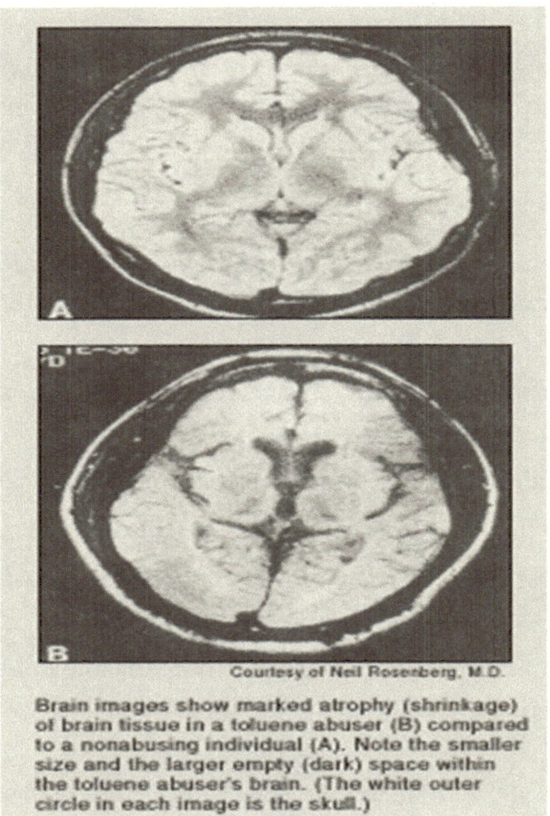

Magnetic Resonance Imaging of brain of an Inhalant abuser

Neurological sequelea -

Encephalopathy - Reversible in early stages of addiction and later it leads to a permanent brain damage.

Ototoxicity - Hearing &equilibrium loss

Oculomotor nerve damage causes nystagmus (rapid involuntary movements of the eyes)

Optic neuritis - with Methyl Ethyl Ketone. Leads to vision defects.

Olfactory nerve – anosmia (loss of sense of smell)

Trigeminal neuropathy.

Axonal degeneration - spasticity (Hexane)

Myelo-neuropathy (defects in the spinal cord and the peripheral nerves)

Peripheral neuropathies (Methyl Butyl Ketone, Hexane) -Loss of temperature, pin prick, touch sensations.

Lungs

Repeated use of inhalants affects the lung parenchyma very profoundly. The lung epithelium gets damaged due to the presence of the chemical. The inhalant also destroys the cilia in the epithelium (the inner lining of the lungs). Oxygen is replaced by the inhalant thus giving rise to hypoxia. The damage compromises oxygen intake by the epithelium even when the individual is not taking the inhalant.

Pulmonary effects also include bronchospasm, asphyxia, acute lung injury (ALI), and aspiration pneumonitis.

There is a sinus discharge, coughing, cyanosis (bluish coloration of lips and tongue), and upper and lower airway irritation.

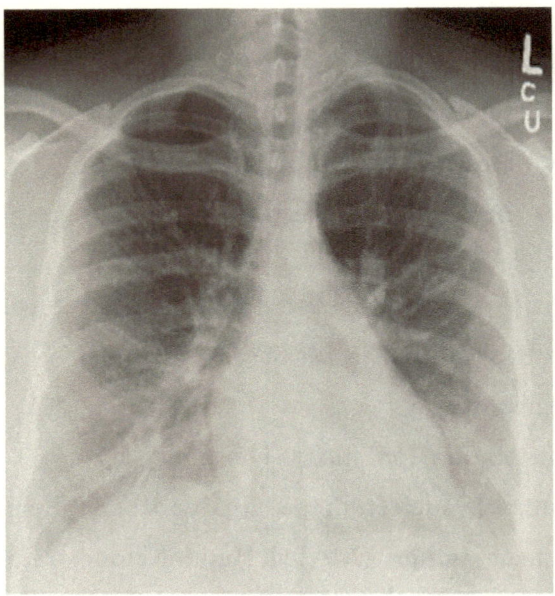

Radiologic view of Lungs in an Inhalant Abuser

Heart

Toluene has direct negative effects on cardiac automaticity and conduction and can sensitize the myocardium to circulating catecholamine.

Heart problems that can occur due to inhalant abuse are irregular heartbeat, first-degree heart block, arrhythmias, and "sudden sniffing death syndrome". Sudden Sniffing Death Syndrome is usually associated with cardiac arrest. The inhalant causes the heart to beat rapidly and erratically, and then resulting in cardiac arrest. This can happen after a long session of sniffing and it can occur in first time users as well.

The long exposure to inhalants leads to heart failure resulting from a persistent irregular heartbeat.

Gastrointestinal

Problems include abdominal pain, nausea, and vomiting. This results from gastric irritation caused by inhalants. Long term use is known to cause gastric ulcers leading to hematemesis (bloody vomiting).

Liver

Liver function can actually shut down, either temporarily or permanently, depending on length and extent of inhalant use.

Hepatotoxicity manifests with ascites (fluid in abdomen), jaundice, hepatomegaly, and liver failure. A rare form of hepatitis—hepatic reticulo-endothelial failure (HREF)—has been reported with toluene exposure. With the widespread abuse of volatile substances in young adults today, hepatitis secondary to toluene toxicity, not just infectious causes, should be considered in the differential diagnosis in the younger patient population who present with concerning findings.

Cirrhosis is the eventual outcome of long exposure to inhalants.

Renal and Metabolic

There is an extreme malnutrition in inhalant abusers which affects the kidney functions severely.

Reported renal toxicity from toluene exposure includes the following:

Renal tubular acidosis (RTA)

Hypokalemia (low levels of potassium)

Hypophosphatemia (low levels of phosphates)

Hyperchloremia (increased levels of chlorides)

Azotemia- high levels of nitrogen compounds as creatinine, urea)

Sterile pyuria.

Hematuria- blood in urine

Proteinuria- proteins in urine

Kidney stones and complete loss of kidney function can develop.

Musculoskeletal

Toluene can affect skeletal muscles directly, resulting in rhabdomyolysis (destruction of muscle mass) and myoglobinemia. Profound hypokalemia due to Renal Tubular Acidosis can produce severe muscle weakness mimicking Guillain-Barre syndrome. In animal studies, chronic inhalational exposure to toluene was found to affect bone metabolism, contributing to bone resorption and inhibition of bone formation.

Long-term inhalant abuse leads to muscle weakness, muscle wasting, and reduced muscle tone and strength.

Hematologic

The blood picture undergoes significant changes.

Hematologic consequences of exposure to inhalants include change in shape, size, and numbers of blood cells and also their functions. Lymphocytosis, macrocytosis, eosinophilia, hypochromic, and basophilic stippling, and in severe cases, aplastic anemia are changes to be seen.

Bone Marrow

Inhalants damage bone marrow. In addition, the chemical benzene, which is found in gasoline, has been shown to cause leukemia.

Dermatologic

Inhalant contact with skin may range in severity from dermatitis to extensive chemical burns with coagulation necrosis.

Peripheral nervous system

Damage from inhalants can cause temporary numbness, permanent nerve damage, permanent paralysis, or generalized weakness, depending on the frequency of abuse. Polyneuropathies can be associated with the use of some inhalants (e.g., nitrous oxide).

Hearing

Some who abuse inhalants become deaf because of chemicals that destroy cells that relay sound to the brain.

Other medical effects

Other effects of inhalant abuse include methemoglobinemia -

Methemoglobinemia (MetHb) is a blood disorder in which an abnormal amount of methemoglobin is produced. Hemoglobin is the protein in red blood cells (RBCs) that carries and distributes oxygen to the body. Methemoglobin is a form of hemoglobin.

With methemoglobinemia, the hemoglobin can carry oxygen, but is not able to release it effectively to body tissues.

Teratogenicity

Fetal damage similar to that observed in patients with "fetal alcohol syndrome". The mothers abusing inhalants deliver babies with microcephaly (small size head), growth retardation and facial dysmorphia. Other features as micrognathia (small sized jaw), low set ears, flat nasal bridge, abnormal scalp hair patterning, down turned corners of the mouth, and large anterior fontanels. Hearing loss and cleft-palate may also be seen.

They have slow development with hyperactivity and disturbed cerebellar (balance and muscle coordination) functions.

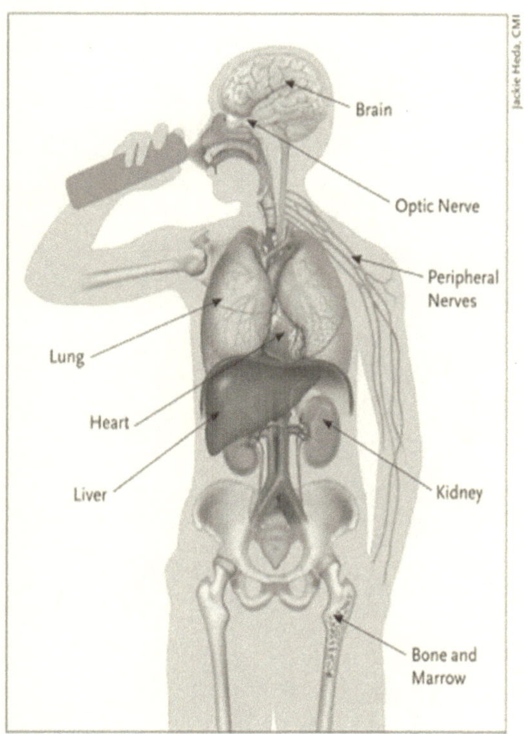

Inhalant Abuse effects on various body systems

Inhalant abuse pattern differs from one country to another. For instance USA witnesses use of whipping cream, air-conditioner gas, and propellants used in cosmetics. In India these are rare for reasons as cheaper drugs are affordable as there is lack of funds and using the above mentioned requires some different skill which the abusers in our country are not aware of as yet.

EPIDEMIOLGICAL STUDY

Data was collected from an exclusive de-addiction center manned with Psychiatrist, social workers, clinical psychologists and laboratory. The center caters to alcohol, heroin and drug addicts. There has been a separate unit for treating street children who have been dependent on inhalants. The center was taking street children in inpatient care. The clients were worked up for assessment of the drug problem, clinical diagnosis, laboratory tests, treatment and rehabilitation.

Data was also collected from other Non-Governmental organizations working with street children rehabilitation.

Data also collected from Psychiatry Out Patient Department of hospital and clinic. The patients who had come for inhalant abuse problem were screened and investigated. They were the mostly walk-in patients and some referred from schools.

SOCIO-DEMOGRAPHIC PROFILE

To study the socio-demographic profile a *semi-structured* proforma was used to record Age, sex, education, economic background, family structure, sibling order, addiction and violence in family.

The data thus collected was put up on statistical analysis and interpretation. I have tried to group the patients who have been under our care into four classes namely- street children, school children, drug-addicts, miscellaneous as motor mechanics, and call center staff.

Age Distribution

The street children are usually from broken homes or homeless, and are the ignored section of any metropolis. They have been ignored by policy makers. They have lived in their own society with their own set of rules. These can be called rules of the jungle where for survival they have to be keen alert fighters with survival instincts. They could otherwise be mute followers who get exploited but have the security of the group that exploits them.

They can be seen hanging around cross-roads often begging or simply whiling away their time. They are commonly found in back alleys, deserted lanes, around dust bins in groups. But they could be seen in the dead of night as well loitering around in the dark, at a time when most of us are in the safe confines of our homes.

They would live off alms given by people or from the money they have got from whatever they have stolen and sold. They would be seen in large numbers outside temples and gurudwaras where they get alms, Prasad or even meals which are enough to quench their appetite for the time being.

Often they would not be at the meal distribution at a specified time and thus they would have to go underfed that day. It matters least for them as they have adapted themselves to sleep off without filled up tummies. They would consume some intoxication or simply smoke bidis (indigenous cigarettes) as this helps them forget their appetite.

By surveys carried out it is quite clear that the population of street children in a big metropolis like Delhi could be at an estimated 1.5 lakhs.

At the tender age that they are compelled to a street life they are exposed to addictions most commonly smoking, cannabis, inhalants and spirit. However inhalants are the most prevalent addiction amongst this section of population being the cheapest and easily available.

They are also exposed to sexual exploration and exploitation.

Street Children

The children were divided age wise into four categories. The following picture comes to the fore.

5-8 years- The youngest inhalant abuser treated at the center was 5 years old. There were many more in this group. They were 6 % of the number of street children admitted.

8-10 years- The next group comprised of grown up boys and girls. They comprised approximately 20% of the population studied.

11-15 years- In this age group we see children who are now teenagers and sexuality is now a very strong driving force. The growth into a man or a girl is most satisfying. The will to be courageous amongst boys accounts for a large number of teen street children going for drugs, inhalants. Nearly 50 % of the street children consuming inhalants come from this group. Girls have by now built a habit of trying out any new intoxicant that comes their way without any contemplation. Many girls would take dangerous intoxicants only to belong to a group.

16-20 years- Children and adolescents from this group account for 22% of inhalant abuser amongst street children. I believe by now the child has grown strong and is capable of getting more money by doing odd jobs or by cheating stealing. He/she is more likely to move out to where grown up children are. They also go in for other addictions besides inhalants. Drugs as cannabis, opium, smack are abused. Alcohol locally made is another option.

School Children

The school going children were divided into three age groups. This was done for convenience as the number of children in the age group of 5 to 10 years had no incidence of inhalant abuse. This does not go to say that there would not be inhalant abusers in this age group of school going children. In our sample which comprised of nearly a 100 students we did not have case reports.

Moreover during this age a child is under very intimate scrutiny and care of parents and teachers and any odd behavior would get noticed.

5-10 years - This group of school going children had no cases reporting of inhalant abuse or any other addiction. However it cannot be ruled out in the current social and family circumstances, where a child witnesses one form or the other of addictions being used in his vicinity. Commonly these being alcohol, cigarettes.

11-15 years- In this age group are children who are in a transitional age. They have entered their teenage and the world is a big experimental, adventure filled playground. The sexual drives, the drive to project an image, fashion, desire to be a cut above the crowd, a desire to be daring, unconventional are all such factors that the as yet immature mind of a teenager cannot handle and is easily swept away. They are likely to try out cigarettes, cannabis or even inhalants.

In the population studied, this group comprised 20 % of the total inhalant abusing school children.

16-20 years- In this age group we have children in late teens that are on the threshold of a career selection, friends, fashion and many more of the issues that they had as younger teens. However now they are stronger, more self- willed and more rebellious. If they have been initiated into drugs earlier or currently they are hell bent about justifying it and every other non-conforming behavior that they have. They are rebellious either covertly or overtly.

This group accounts for nearly 80% of the total drug abusing population amongst school going children.

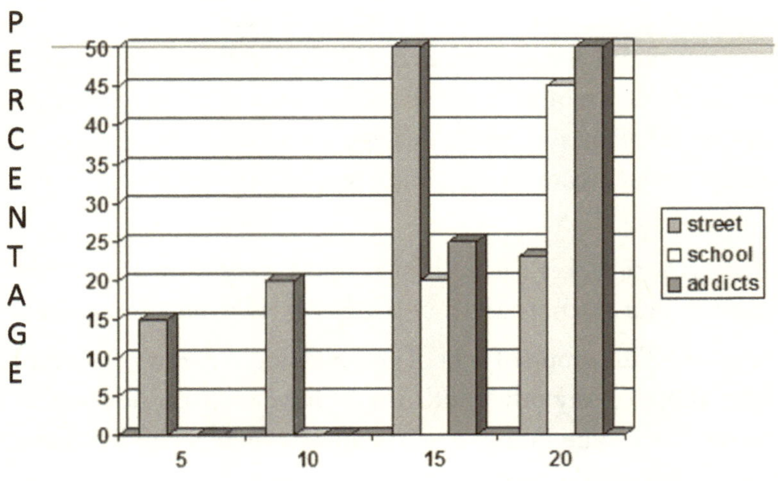

Call Centre Staff

20 years and above. These are employed individuals who have shift duties to attend to their foreign clients. A typical call center staff attends to 100 to 150 calls per day and has to be accurate in his information and dealing with the telephonic client on the other side of the world. It does tend to become very stressful most of the times especially when the staff is doing duty in the graveyard hours.

These individuals are youngsters who have joined call center job as a stop gap measure, as a fill-in till such time that they get a job suited to their qualifications and aptitude. Most individuals take their pay as a pocket money and want to live it up.

Most of these individuals want to party to beat the stress. They as youngsters have their own groups. Taking alcohol is common but some of them prefer taking cannabis, cough syrup, or inhalants. Individually as well some take a break from the taxing call-taking and go for a joint of "grass". As one client of mine reported – he would take regular breaks as everyone else did after an hour or more. In this break there is a big "no – no" to coffee for him but a few deep sniffs of the inhalant, or a smoke, or doing grass is what he regularly does.

Male to female distribution not done as females did not report for treatment from a call center. The friends of these female dependents have given vivid accounts of female carrying typewriter fluids to take their regular sniffs while on duty and off duty. It had been easy for them to carry the inhalants in their bags.

Most of these "addicts" get over the habit as they get better jobs and there is a change in their circle. However very few do stick to "once in a while kick" on inhalants in later life. Others would take alcohol on a regular basis.

There is no clear cut statistical record and a good idea would be to take a survey of call centers to understand the pattern of drug abuse.

Motor Mechanics

10-15 years- Amongst the motor mechanics this is the age group that has inhalant abusers. They have been initiated into this dependence by a senior mechanic or just as an exploration since a few get to like the smell of glue, petrol or other things as grease or lubricants readily available at the garage.

What begins as a curiosity goes on to become a habit and finally an unquenchable need. Thus dependence follows. This habit makes them groggy uncoordinated and confused. This behavior comes in the way of their functioning and mistakes are likely to happen, sometimes even serious ones. That is the time they get fired or they come for medical aid. Usually they are brought by their employers.

The parents too notice grossly changed behavior, blood shot drunken eyes, strange smell of inhalants and many other signs which are unmistakable and alarming enough to withdraw the child from the profession and seek medical help.

I have not seen clients beyond 20 years of age reporting with this problem amongst the motor mechanics.

Drug-Addict

5-10 years- none reported in this age group as we don't get to see hard core drug dependents in this age group. Addicts in their childhood are not presenting with severe drug problems. Yes, as mentioned earlier drug addicts in their childhood may be found smoking cigarettes especially in their late childhood. Amongst the addicts the age of reporting with problems of drug abuse is during teens. We therefore get to see addicts during their teenage and later on in adulthood, middle ages. Retrospectively we may get a history of inhalant abuse in late childhood.

In some addicts the inhalant abuse persists even beyond childhood when one regularly or occasionally or for pure monetary reasons still uses them, but for others the journey makes them go in for heavier drugs.

13-15 years- Amongst the addicts studied 22 % were abusing inhalants in addition to other drugs.

15-20 years. In this age group 58 % were those who used inhalants off and on, sometimes as an add-on to bolster their high and at other times for the sheer convenience that goes with using inhalants.

20 years and above– *These individuals have matured deep into addiction and most are by now using 3 to 4 drugs at any point of time. Inhalants are used by them only to boost their high. They sometimes use inhalants as it provides a cheap replacement for some drug which they may not have been able to procure. They comprise the remaining20 % of the population amongst drug addicts.*

Education

EDUCATION

	Street Children	School Children	Motor Mechanics	Drug Addict
Illiterate- 54.7 %	----	8%	3%
5 th Std- 33.5%	----	65%	31%
5-8 Std - 9.5%	-----	15 %	30%
8-10 Std- ----	25 %	10 %	21%
10-12 Std ----	75 %	02%	15%
Graduate----			

The above table shows the educational status of the different groups studied

The table is discussed below.

Educational Status in Street Children

The street children population presents a very dismal picture. This is expected as this population is without home or out of home, poor, with no access to any minimum government plans. Those lucky few who make it to shelters and homes do not get to study. The quality of life is sub-standard and despite many programs to rehabilitate them they don't seem to receive these. They always stand a neglected lot of any metropolis population.

Getting to have two square meals and basic health amenities is a privileged thing for them, studies and education is simply not imaginable.

Days pass into weeks, weeks into months, and months into years and years into decades the street life style persists and this life revolves around need for food, safety and addictions in any form (inhalants).

Hygiene, love, compassion and education have never figured in their list of necessary things as the street life is too challenging to let them focus on anything else for a long time. Momentarily they yearn for a home, good clothes, love, belonging and a good life.

They witness good life all around them when they see life passing by, when they see happy children, happy people and other good things of life.

As expected since they have left their homes at a tender age they are not educated.

Amongst the inhalant taking street children:

- Fifty seven (57) % were illiterate.

- Thirty three point five (33.5) % were educated up to fifth standard.

- Nine point five (9.5) % had studied up to eighth standard till they dropped out of school or left their homes.

On interviewing these children to find out cause of poor education following facts came out.

- They were getting physically assaulted and abused often beaten mercilessly and to escape the wrath of a demonical guardian they ran away from their homes.

- They were forcibly taken out of school on the pretext that the child should work to contribute to family income. Usually such was the case when the guardian was himself addicted to alcohol, opium, or hashish and needed money to sustain his/her habit.

- The addict guardian would also cut down on expenses as clothes, food just to sustain their own habit.

- The family atmosphere was one of a disturbed family with abusive, aggressive and disruptive behavior which was not conducive to studying.

- And once on the streets the child would make friends who sooner than later introduced them to drugs.

Educational Status of School Going Children

Amongst the school going children the distribution of inhalant (drug) taking population is as follows:

- Twenty five (25) % were from fifth to eighth standard.
- Seventy five (75) % were from ninth to twelfth standard.

The causes of taking to drugs in general in school going children have been highlighted earlier in the chapters on reasons for taking drugs.

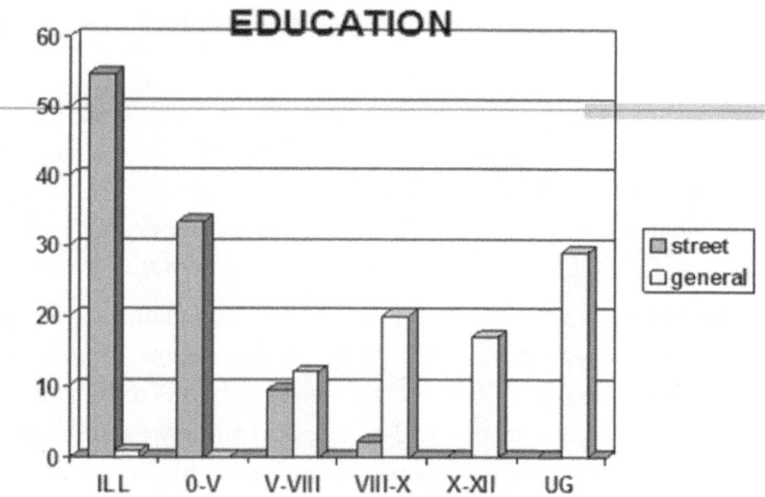

ILL- ILLITERATE, 0-V : UPTO FIFTH CLASS, V-VIII: FIFTH TO EIGHTH, VIII-X UPTO TENTH, X-XII: UPTO TWELFTH, UG: UNDERGRADUATE

Educational Status in Motor Mechanics

Amongst the boys and the teens or young adults who take to the profession of a motor mechanic there is always a very pressing need for money for family. The children whom we see getting trained or working at the mechanics are the ones who have to contribute to the family income. In this process they forego many things that were due to them in their childhood. These being education, playtime, video games, fun and fashion. Thus very high education is not seen and the distribution of educational category would be as follows.

- Illiterate compose eight (8) % of the inhalant abusers in this class

- The major chunk of addicts had studied up to fifth standard. These being sixty five (65) %. One could try to explain this peculiar phenomenon. One explanation that comes to my mind is that in this class of people children below ten years are considered really small and the moment they have touched ten years plus they are regarded as now growing up. Thus the biological categorization of a child till twelve years of age does not hold good.

- So mostly children who have studied up to fifth class (around 10 to 11 years) are taken into some profession and have to leave their education.

- A passing comment even though girls are not seen as motor mechanics is that girls are considered grown up and capable of taking care of household responsibilities as they enter their teens in uneducated classes, and people with orthodox view of life(villagers/ city dwellers). Thus they are also forcibly taken out of schools.

- Nearly fifteen (15) % of the inhalant abuser mechanics had studied up to eighth standard. Here too similar factors as mentioned before are operative. The need for working hands to bolster family earnings is the major reason. The need for money could be because of sudden rise in family expenses due to infirmity, death, marriage of a daughter or even a drunken father.

- About ten (10) % of the inhalant abusers amongst motor mechanics had an education up to tenth standard.

- Another two (2) % of motor mechanics had apparently finished their schooling or were in their twelfth standard when they had to leave their studies. In all these cases the pressing need for money has been a strong factor.

- However in some cases the child could not pull on with studies as he had got into bad company, or the student had lost interest in studies or was not having an aptitude for studying further.

- Often the father owns a garage and initiates the boy to drop school and learn the trade. However nowadays people do want their children to do graduation even if it has to be from open universities.

Educational Status in Addict Population

Classifying a certain population as addict population can be misleading as we are studying addicts who are addicted to other drugs as cannabis, opiates, alcohol, tablets and in addition have started taking inhalants either from the past or currently.

Thus addicts who have come for treatment of inhalant abuse have been older individuals and not children. These are individuals who have reported a long history of multiple drug abuse other than inhalants for a fairly long time. Somewhere down the line they experimented with inhalants and are now dangerously dependent on it.

The educational background of addicts is as detailed below.

- Three (3) % were illiterate.

- Thirty one (31) % had studied up to fifth standard.

- Thirty (30) % had schooling up to eighth standard.

In the addict group of people monetary constraints have not been the major reason for giving up studies. Other factors as broken family, addiction in the family, friends using inhalants/drugs are the major contributing factors.

Children who have dropped out of school have done so due to drug taking behavior coupled with lack of family control, concern and support.

- Twenty one (21) % had completed up to tenth to twelfth standard.

This being a stressful time for students as they have to plan for their future career, drugs provide an escape route for this. Persons who were already on drugs lose sight of their goals and focus in life. They get sucked into an addict routine of taking drugs and then taking more drugs.

- Fifteen (15) % had *completed their high schools or graduation at college.*

Sex Distribution

The drug scene in any metropolis has a preponderance of males in comparison to females. It has always been like that. Boys are more risk taking and girls are cautious and generally fearful inherently. Girls also do not come out openly when they are into drug scene.

The pub scene and rave parties are seeing girls in large numbers these days which is a very grim picture of the problem. It reflects many things from the girls needs to self-assertion, to a need to have equal opportunities and freedom, to a need to belong to a group, to rebel against their social norms which they find very oppressing. This could also be a reflection of a serious mental disorder, or a result of a stressful atmosphere.

Headlines in tabloids give us an idea of the rave parties happening in a most secretive manner. Right from arrangement of party drugs, to a secret location everything is hidden under a cover.

Rave party busted in Dehradun, 25 boys and 14 girls arrested: December 2, 2012.

44 boys and 4 girls detained from a rave party in Gurgaon: December 26, 2014.

Rave party busted as police raid a posh hotel, 27 boys and 6 girls: 16 February, 2016.

Such headlines are very common these days and indicate that girls from affluent classes and upper middle class are taking drugs in large numbers.

Taking alcohol as wine, beer or even hard drink is the accepted norm with the new generation.

People who have attended rave parties have used very high end designer drugs along with known ones as cannabis, cocaine, heroin, inhalants and many more. You don't have rave parties every day and therefore one has to get on with other drug including inhalants on other days.

Inhalant abuse being an easy to use option has many takers amongst girls especially those attending schools or offices. However a clear number of girls to boy's ratio are not possible to evaluate in the general population. We can only infer from the data that presents to us in our de addiction hospital or clinic set- ups.

The distribution on the basis of sex is given below. The figure for boys is a good representation of the addiction amongst boys. The actual number of girls goes unreported and also girls are under lot of social stigma which they have to face in some societies.

School Children Male: Female Ratio

The male/female distribution is 98 % to 2%. This is considering that many girls are going unreported even in the schools. The parents are hesitant to report any abnormalities to the school or the doctor. Only the close friends of the girl know about her addiction and they are loyal enough not to divulge it to a stranger. Often it is the addict boys who form the close circle of the girl addict.

The number of girls reporting would be much less than the actual number of girls affected.

Street Children Male: Female Ratio

The distribution of male/female is 95 % boys to 5 % girls. Here very interestingly nearly 70 to 80 % of girls among the street children population are hooked onto the inhalants. And 99 % are dependent on nicotine. Few are cannabis users.

The girls are a vulnerable lot on the street. They have to follow the leader and do things they (the girls) may not actually want to do. Drugs are only one face of exploitation the other one is sexual exploitation. A girl has to protect herself therefore she befriends the group members to be secured.

Call Center Workers Male: Female Ratio

The accurate picture is not available as the number of girls taking inhalants are for all practical purposes not visible. They are very secretive about it. We therefore do not know their distribution. What we can gather from the boys coming from call centers for consultation is that there are is a significant number of girls who take inhalants regularly. The exact numbers they too can't give.

So no reliable data to highlight sex distribution.

Addicts Male: Female Ratio

Amongst the addict population the distribution is 97 % of boys to 3 % of girls. This picture is not quite specific as many girls abusing drugs go undeclared. The girls who come for treatment are already addicted to hard drugs as heroin, and using routinely alcohol or cannabis. On detailed questioning the pattern of abuse is revealed.

This is a serious issue that amongst addict as well the number of girls reporting for treatment is substantially less than the actual numbers. Girls do not come early for treatment. There is lot of stigma which compels them to be in hiding till matters go worse.

Inhalant Abuse Pattern

Included data is based on the observation of types of Inhalants used primarily. Details of drugs used secondarily in addition to the inhalants. Often the primary drugs have been nicotine or alcohol and the patient has subsequently started using inhalant in large amounts and most of the time. Mostly the picture has been of poly drug abuse. The current status has more inhalant abuse of the many drugs the patient is using

INHALANT ABUSE PROFILE

	Street Children	School Children	Drug Dependants
One Drug - NIL	10%	-----
Two Drug – 17%	40%	8%
Three Drug- 7%	50%	42%
Four Drug- 30%	-----	50%
Multiple Drugs-45 %		

The pattern of poly drug abuse is detailed in subsequent paragraphs based on a meticulous observation taking into consideration the history of length of use of the drugs abused and the current preferred drug of abuse.

Street Children Drug Abuse Profile

Mostly the addiction to any substance of abuse starts with cigarettes and or bidis (indigenous smoking sticks). The addiction to cigarettes and bidis is not put up in the statistical account as this was common in all addictions as a routine. The street children start experimentally and once hooked onto it (cigarettes) tend to use it regularly along with other newer drugs that they may try out later on.

So finding a person taking only cigarettes was not there the study as we are not studying the phenomena of nicotine abuse. And finding someone who was using only inhalants was not there amongst street children as mostly all those who had started with cigarettes eventually had problem of inhalant abuse as well on their hands.

Only 17 % (seventeen) of street children were dependent on two drugs the inhalants and cigarettes/bidis at the time of collecting the data. Sooner or later they would abuse alcohol, cannabis without getting addicted to it. Subsequently they would get dependent on other drugs as mentioned.

It is a very large percentage, given the hostile environment the street children are exposed to. To be dependent on only inhalants or only cigarettes is a rarity.

Seven percent (7 %) of street children eventually present with cigarette and two drug abuse. Mostly it is cigarettes, inhalants and alcohol; or cigarettes, inhalants and cannabis. Use of inhalants, cannabis and cigarettes is fairly common and affordable.

Thirty percent (30 %) of street children are dependent on more than two drugs. The three drugs in various combinations are

Inhalants + cigarettes + cannabis + alcohol: this is the most prevalent poly drug abuse. It happens to be affordable. You may wonder that alcohol would cost the patient a good sum of money. Well it becomes accessible as the seniors in the street do the younger one favor of this kind in exchange of small errands or sexual gratification or the juniors themselves procure money by dubious means to purchase liquor.

Inhalants + cannabis + heroin + cigarettes: This is a more expensive combination. Heroin is costly and person dependent is not very keen to share it. Especially as the withdrawal symptoms of heroin are very painful the addict wants to avoid it at all cost. Thus they do not share their emergency quota of heroin which helps them tide over the withdrawal period.

Inhalants + cannabis + opium + cigarettes: This pattern of drug abuse is comparatively less costly than the combination with heroin. It however is not preferred by all as the kick is much less with opium. Often opium is consumed to abort withdrawal symptoms of heroin which the patient might be taking.

Inhalants + opium + cigarettes + alcohol: The dependence to this combination of drugs is not very common. Again it's the cost of alcohol that requires to be arranged to make it a regular affair.

Inhalants+ smack + cigarettes + alcohol: As with the above pattern this combination too is expensive and less percentage of street children take to it. Eventually many street children switch over to other combinations which are easier to procure and less costly.

The interchanging of various secondarily used drugs that is jumping from heroin to smack to alcohol to cannabis is under following circumstances:

- The choice of secondary drugs is not available

- Not enough money to buy the preferred drug(primary addiction)

- Usually a loose pattern of secondary addiction. The individual takes any drug that comes his/her way with no special preference. These individuals move with the mood of their crowd and are adjusting and non-asserting. OR They are desperate to keep their high at any cost by taking any drug. They are exposed to serious hazards and risk taking that could prove dangerous.

Multiple drug abuse- Nearly forty five percent (45 %) of the street children is multiple drug abusers. Going by our analysis they are consuming more than four drugs at any point of time. These individuals are taking sedative pills, pain killer tablets which belong to opiate class and cough syrups. Thus they are taking any of the combinations mentioned under the head of four drug abuses that is inhalants, cigarettes, alcohol, cannabis, opium, heroin, and smack along with pills or cough syrups.

Essentially the longer a person lives on the streets the more likely he/she is to follow a pattern of poly drug abuse.

School Children Drug Abuse Profile

Single drug abuse: About ten percent (10 %) of school children reporting for treatment had one drug problem that is abusing inhalants only. This presented as occasional use in school which would go unnoticed. Using inhalants at home led to prominent signs of inhalant abuse being easily noticed.

Two drug abuse: Nearly forty percent (40 %) of school children reporting for addiction issues had a history of taking two drugs. Generally this was cigarettes and inhalants. This group was the ones who had started on cigarettes much before they tried inhalants and then presented with dual addiction.

Some presenting with dual addiction were consuming inhalants regularly and alcohol occasionally.

A good number had addiction to inhalants with consuming cough syrups.

The numbers reporting for treatment have been few thus the distribution of these patterns of dual addiction cannot be classified into most prevalent to least prevalent.

Three drug abuse: The school children belonging to this group are seniors from higher classes. They have had a long history of taking cigarettes and trying out other drugs. They comprise a major fifty percent (50 %) of the total school kids presenting with drug problems. Usually the various drugs commonly used are-

- Cigarettes, cannabis, and Inhalants
- Cigarettes, alcohol and Inhalants
- Cigarettes, cannabis, alcohol and Inhalants
- Cigarettes, cough syrups and Inhalants
- Cigarettes, cannabis, cough syrups and Inhalants
- Some would use more than four of the drugs mentioned above concurrently.

We have a larger problem at hand as many school students do not report for medical help. Many girls try out inhalants for the sheer quick kick that it offers. Additionally it is convenient and untraceable in the initial phases.

The undetected cases finally come up later on with poly drug abuse or medical complications.

Drug Addict Population Drug Abuse Profile

This statistical account includes the addict populations who have later on started using inhalants as a recreational drug. Their primary drug of abuse had been heroin/cannabis/cough syrups/alcohol/others.

Amongst the addict population distribution is as follows:

- One drug abuse – NIL

- Two drug abuse – NIL. An addict using cigarettes and inhalants is primarily classified as an inhalant abuser. A cannabis dependent taking inhalant is actually using three drugs that are cigarettes, cannabis and inhalants.

- Three drug abuse- eight percent of drug addicts who had started using inhalants had a history of using two drugs in the past. These being-

  Cigarette + cannabis and later inhalants

  Cigarette + cough syrup, later inhalants

  Cigarette + brown sugar, later on inhalants abuse

  Cigarette + alcohol and later inhalants

  The above combination shows a choice preference from the most preferred to the least preferred choice.

- Four drug abuses – Forty two percent (42 %) of drug addicts who reported for inhalant dependence currently along with other substance abuse had a four drug abuse pattern.

  This would be

  Cigarettes + cannabis + cough syrup later they started inhalants as well.

Cigarettes + cannabis + brown sugar and later on inhalants

Cigarettes + cannabis + alcohol then inhalants

Cigarettes + cough syrup + alcohol then inhalants

Cigarettes + opium + alcohol and later on inhalants.

Four plus drug abuse – Fifty percent (50%) of the drug addict population that presented for consultation had a pattern of abusing more than four drugs in addition to inhalants. Inhalants had never been a primary addiction in these cases. They tried out inhalants in company, and would later on use it for reasons of cost, quick action, and easy procurability.

The pattern is essentially as seen in four drug abuse but additionally these individuals are hooked on to taking tablets, injectable as listed below-

Dextropropoxyphene capsules

Sleeping pills as diazepam, Nitrazepam, clonazepam etcetera.

Codeine phosphate tablets

Methaqualone tablets, amphetamines, cocaine, crax (adulterated cocaine), LSD

Injectable buprenorphine, pentazocine, diazepam, morphine or improvised heroin, smack and or dextro-propoxyphene capsule injections. Injectable use of cocaine, mephedrone is reported amongst the addicts who are well off and can afford it.

The longer the history of addiction longer is the list of drugs abused by an addict.

Socio-Economic Background

Street Children Socio- Economic Status

Amongst the street children with inhalant abuse problem who were at our center the distribution as per socio-economic background was as follows.

- Seventy three percent (73 %) were from poor class. Usually the parents were having meager income and many mouths to feed. In addition the family would be having an extra burden on the purse in the form of sickness of a family member, marriage of a daughter.

- Twenty four percent (24 %) of the patients from the street have been from lower middle class. Usually in these cases the family environment has been the second major factor forcing the kids to run away from home as we shall discuss later while dealing with family structure and related issues.

- Three percent (3 %) of the street children has been from middle class background. Surprisingly middle class has an admiringly stable integrated family structure in India. But here we get to see many such triggers in families which compel the kids to run away from their homes. The various unfavorable factors are discussed in the later chapters.

- We had no children from the upper middle or upper class amongst street children population.

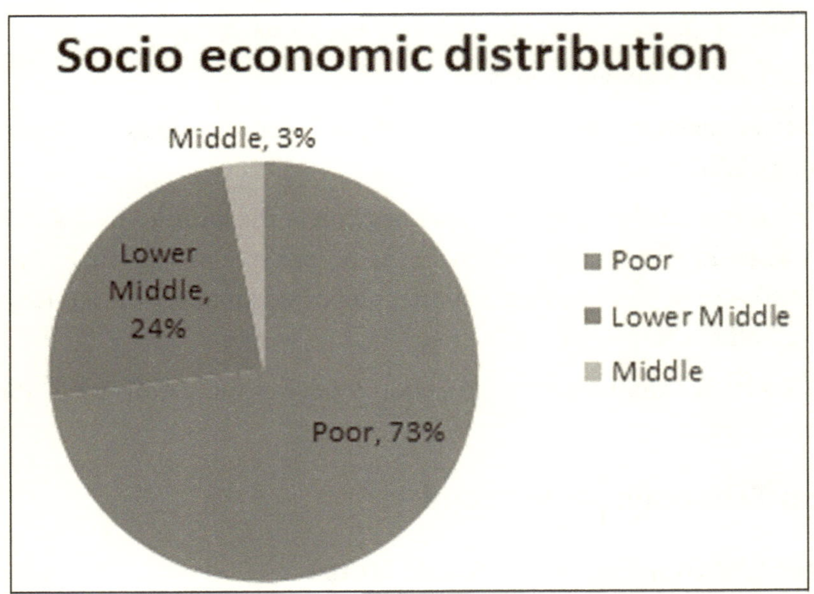

School Children Socio-Economic Background

Different Schools are broadly catering to different socio-economic class .Thus there are affluent high end schools for the very rich and powerful. Schools catering to middle class and upper middle class are many and Government run schools cater to middle and lower income group.

Under special provisions from the government now, it has become mandatory for private and public schools to admit children from deprived classes usually free of cost.

No accurate data can be claimed from any of these schools. Mostly data is collected from friends and students who themselves may not be using. Users avoid reporting to medical units in the schools as it brings bad name to them and their family. They also face ostracization in the school in subtle or very obvious ways from fellow students and few staff.

I have treated cannabis, smack abusers from high end schools in Delhi at my clinic. On probing them we found out that they had tried out inhalants sometimes and especially as *fillers in between* for their preferred intoxicant. It was also used by them while attending classes as it was easy to use and not detectable.

Drug usage seems to be more prevalent in high end schools. Many students are seen flocking together in forlorn areas of the schools. These students usually stay aloof from the rest of the crowd. Whenever one of these students (client) came for treatment of drug problem and recovered he would refer other friends and users to my clinic for treatment. Thereafter we would get regular clients who have been in the drug abusing circle of friends.

Later on another cliché of boys and girls would trickle in for treatment of their drug problem. Inhalants were very rare in these patients which had got treatment in the 1990s. The subsequent decade saw a rise in inhalant abuse amongst school children in a noticeable way. There are no accurate statistical data on this count. One can discern the difference in the addiction patterns of the clients who report for treatment.

Drug taking behavior has been palpably present in some schools and in some it has been a menace. These schools had to involve parents to sort out the issues. Some students had to leave the school and had been issued transfer certificates. This refers to a prestigious school in Delhi. Some schools often get in news these days for all the wrong reasons.

This is another very prestigious school in Delhi No statistical data accurately describes the problem in schools however schools are taking steps to tackle the drug abuse problem head on. They have initiated a program with the help of NARCONON and UNODC.

I have been associated with a school that caters to students from middle and upper middle income group. However students from economically weaker sections (EWS) are also there in large numbers. These schools have to comply with government directives to give admissions to these students from (EWS) categories in a sizeable number. The said school and many others are the ones that have been given land by the government at concessional rates hence they have to comply with the directives.

In spite of the population profile of the students which represents all sections of society in this school there were no cases reporting with a problem of inhalant abuse or for that matter even drug/cannabis abuse. No students reported for treatment. Those who had a problem with drugs or inhalants remained behind curtains. Their friends and other students could give an idea of how many users was there in their class. The seriously addicted were sent for consultation and treatment to my clinic and other appropriate centers dealing with drug addictions.

One can estimate that most cases that fall victim to drugs, inhalants are from upper middle class, upper class and lower class. The incidence seems marginally in middle class. The inhalant abuse is seen across all sections of society.

Family Structure

The family structure bears a very pivotal role in any one's life. It holds the key to good nurturing, grooming, sense of security and happiness for the present and future. The family shapes the behavior of the members by the profound influence it has on them not only in what it provides whether good or bad but also what it fails to provide.

A family provides economic, physical and mental support and that special emotional support that special warmth which gives growth and a sense of well –being to an individual. It heals all ills that plague us. A family has to be a place where one is accepted unconditionally even when one has nowhere else to go. In spite of all our draw backs a family assimilates us. This is the place where we get a feeling of belonging. We belong to the family and the family belongs to us.

A healthy family has to be having all essentials of complete parenting. This means that both healthy parents should be together as a family. The role of the fathers as a support and the mother's role as a support are felt distinctly by the children. Both the supports are desired and cherished by the children. Jointly too the parents act in unison and the strong coherence between them unites the family into a unitary whole. These characteristics of the parents are assimilated by the children and help them grow into mentally stable and healthy individuals.

The separated parents, single parent families are compromised in dispensing their roles. The gaps in their roles as healthy parents are inevitable. This compromises the child upbringing. The children in such families grow with inadequacies in some aspects of their personalities.

In our study we have found predisposition of certain family structures which are prone to rear up children who later develop misadjusting pattern. The children from these families are more likely to fall victim to errant behavior, anti-social and drug taking behavior.

The families of those who reported to the center for inhalant abuse problems were studied in their completeness. We had focused on families where parents were missing either as a result of death, separation, abandonment or divorce. The influence of incomplete families reflected directly in the incidence of errant, antisocial or drug taking behavior.

Street Children's' Family Structure

Amongst the street children who were admitted for de-addiction the following was seen:

Both Parents Living

- 65 % of Street Children had both parents living. Their families were complete. There were other factors that contributed to their behavior as we shall see in the subsequent deliberations.

Both Parents Dead

- 9.7 % of Street Children were those whose both parents were dead and they had been reared up by foster parents or relatives. They were a hugely neglected lot especially as majority was from poor sections of the society.

Fathers Dead

- 9.7 % of the Street Children were those who had lost their father in early life and were reared up by their mothers alone. They had their own hardships.

Mothers Dead

- 16 % of the Street Children were those who had lost their mothers in their infancy or early childhood. This statistical account is very interesting.

  Discussion: In cases where fathers had died the mothers took care of the children rather properly even after adverse circumstances due to passing away of the husband.

  However where only fathers had to bring up the children after the death of their spouse they had shown marked dereliction of their responsibilities. Under their care the children became prone to abnormal habits, abnormal behavior patterns and erratic life.

  The fathers in these families were never closely attached to its members, they were found to be dependent on some intoxicant or the other.

School Going Children's Family Structure

The following trend was seen in the school children population who had reported for treatment.

Both Parents Living

- 82 % of School Children had both parents living. There would be other factors which have contributed to their addictive behavior as we shall see in the subsequent discussions.

Both Parents Dead

- 3 % of School Children had the upbringing without their parents as they had lost their parents in early life. Their upbringing had been by their relatives.

Father Dead

- 7 % of School going children had lost their fathers and were brought by their mothers as a single parent

Mother Dead

- 8 % of School children had lost their mothers in early infancy or childhood and had been brought by their fathers.

Discussion

The parenting by single parents has shown similar standards of responsibility and comparability of outcomes whether it was father or mother who was bringing up the child after the demise of the spouse.

Drug Addict Family Structure

Amongst the drug addicts the family structure showed the following distribution

Both Parents Living

- 70 % of Drug addicts came from structured families with both parents living. There were other factors that were responsible for the waywardness of the child. Factors that would have been a constant source of stress. Maybe factors related to the members of the family. These would be discussed in the subsequent chapters.

Both Parents Dead

- 3.5 % of Drug addicts taking inhalants and who had reported for treatment were orphans. Both parents had died around crucial years of development in infancy, childhood or teens. The age of losing the parents could be another subject to further research.

Fathers Dead

- 23 % of Drug Addicts who were taking inhalants in addition to other drugs had lost their father early in life. Almost a quarter of the sample amongst the drug addicts is a very large number. This would indicate that losing the father as a parent has a deep impact on an individual's life. The loss affected the economics, the discipline of the family very deeply and mothers alone failed to take care of issues specially the ones related to the child's addiction as she must have had to attend to other issues as finance.

Mothers Dead

- 2 % of Drug Addicts had lost their mothers. This finding raises some questions. One very obvious is how is it that fathers alone have reared up their children safely from getting exposed and addicted to drugs in a much better way whereas mothers have not (compare with rearing outcomes (in street children population) where fathers had died earlier and mothers had to singlehandedly rear up the children).

- Another pertinent issue relates to the class.

We see highly disturbed families that produce addicts whether they come from good or other economic backgrounds. Similarly patients who have come from the streets have unhealthy/disturbed family structures in addition to very poor backgrounds.

The school going children have very healthy family support system and good economic backgrounds which holds them in good stead in the event of loss of a parent.

FAMILY STRUCTURE

	Both Living	Both Dead	Father Dead	Mother Dead
Street Children-School	65%	9.7%	9.7%	16%
Children-	82%	3%	7%	8%
Drug - Dependants	70%	3.5%	23%	2.0%

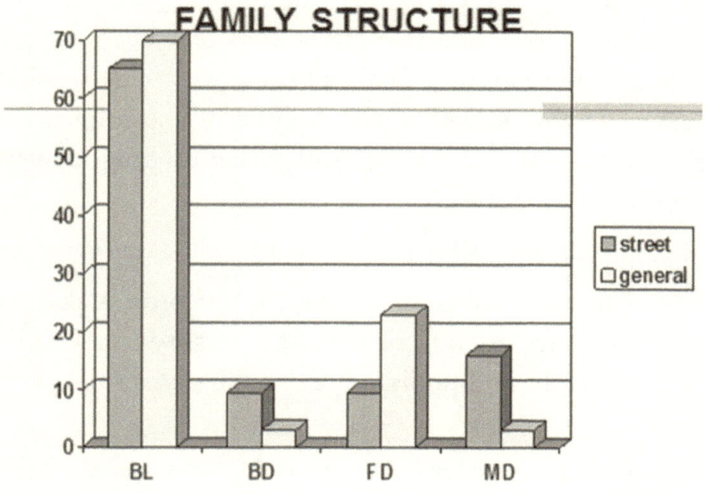

BL- BOTH LIVING   BD- BOTH DEAD   FD- FATHER DEAD   MD- MOTHER DEAD

Sibling Order in Family

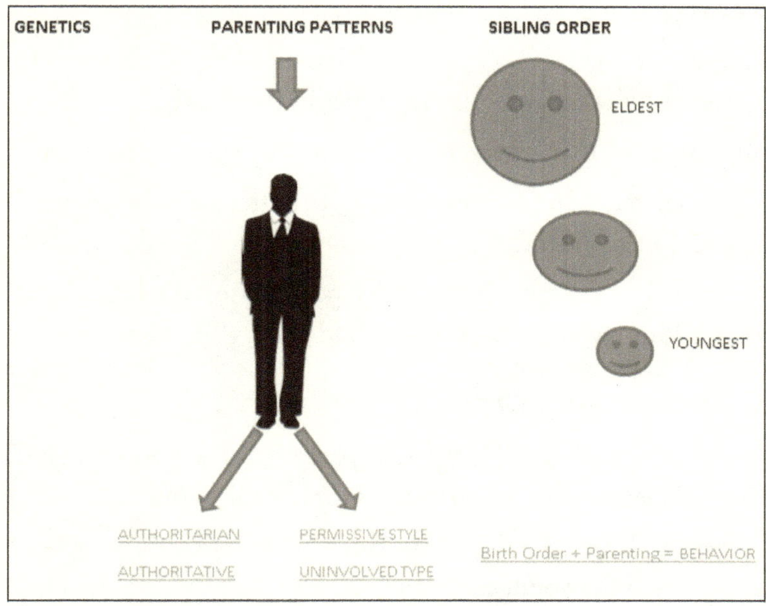

SIBLING ORDER IN FAMILY – A contributing factor in personality development

In our experience while treating drug addicts, inhalant abusers and psychiatric illnesses we found interesting facts related to the position of the individual in the family. Whether he/she were eldest, middle order or youngest child this turned out to be one of the influencing factors responsible for the way a person behaves including drug taking behavior and even psychiatric illnesses.

The sibling order or the birth order as it is called was studied.

What is birth order? Birth order refers to the order a child is born in their family; first-born, second-born or last born are examples. Birth order is often believed to have a profound and lasting effect on psychological development.

In addition to birth order being the only child and its effect on the individual's drug taking behavior was also studied.

Street Children Birth Order

- Eldest sibling: 30 %(Thirty percent) of street children who were taking drugs were eldest child in their family.

- Youngest sibling: 25 %(Twenty five percent) amongst the street children population were the youngest in the family.

- Only son: 3 %(Three percent) were the only sons in their family.

- Only daughter: 2 % (Two percent) of the street children were the only daughter in their family.

- Middle order sibling: 40 %(Forty percent) of the inhalant abusing street children were middle order children in their family.

School Children Birth Order

- Eldest sibling: 35 %(Thirty five percent) of school going children taking inhalants were the eldest sibling in their family.

- Youngest sibling: 23 %(Twenty three percent) amongst school going children were the youngest in their family.

- Only son: 4 %(Four percent) of the school going children were the only son in their families.

- Only daughter: 2 %(Two percent) of the school going inhalant abusers were the only daughters in their families.

- Middle order sibling: 36 %(Thirty six percent) of the school going children taking inhalants were the middle order siblings in their family.

Drug Addicts Birth Order

- Eldest sibling: 30 %(Thirty percent) of patients having drug dependence in addition to inhalant abuse were the eldest sibling in the family.

- Youngest sibling: 32 %(Thirty two percent) of the drug dependents abusing inhalants were the youngest child in their family.

- Only son: 2 %(Two percent) of the drug dependents were the only son in the family.

- Only daughter: 2 %(Two percent) of the drug addicts concurrently abusing inhalants were the only daughters in their family.

- Middle order siblings: 34 %(Thirty four percent) of drug dependents were the middle order siblings in their families.

SIBLING ORDER

	Eldest Son	Youngest Son	Only Son	Only Daughter
Street Children-School	30%	25%	3%	2%
Children-Drug - Dependents	35%	23%	4%	2%
	30%	32%	2%	2%

Discussion

Sibling order or the birth order has a profound effect on an individual's behavior when other predisposing factors are present in their social milieu. Hypothetically it would mean that the birth order itself does not contribute to abnormalities in behavior unless a definitely influencing social environment with its psychological dynamics is provided which shapes the thinking and behavior of the individual.

Let's say a child in a particular birth order is brought up in a hostel, away from the influences of his family and social background then his behavior would differ from another child who has been brought up in his own specific socio-cultural milieu. Because each socio-cultural milieu has attitudes, values, customs which is imparted to the children born in their fold. These particular attitudes and behavior get ingrained during rearing up and carry on into all stages of the individual's life.

Thus the eldest sibling would get importance, responsibilities whether he can shoulder them or not. The attitude and expectations of the family and even the society persists despite the fact that the individual may not be equipped with the necessary capabilities to shoulder and execute such responsibilities.

There can be many shortcomings in any individual. The family members, relatives cannot give up their attitudes towards the individual. These are very hard grained into the psyche of the family members. Not once they introspect that their expectations from the individual is causing distress to the individual.

Eldest born son is looked upon as the second in command next to the father. He has to take responsibilities, in absence of father as well and he is often regarded as a father figure in many cultures. He is consulted for all decisions. He is given due regard in his relative circle and is exposed to critical bickering if he falters anytime or falls short of what is expected of him.

This is often very challenging, frustrating and a burden one wants to ignore. The stresses associated with being the eldest sibling finds channels to vent these frustrations out. And mostly so it is reflected in a sulking behavior, an aggressive selfish behavior, or a refuge in alcohol or drugs.

Eldest born daughter in a metropolis setting could also assume such importance. This is usually due to her grit rather than due to dictum or a custom. The role of being the eldest sibling is not very defined for a girl child in certain orthodox customs. It is customary for the girls to get married and live their life with their husbands and in-laws. However the girls naturally are more concerned towards the parents and siblings so they assume role as the one in-charge of affairs in the house.

Often the second son could be given the position of responsibility if the eldest sibling is a daughter.

Youngest child (son) gets a large share of love doled out to him by one and all that is the family members and the relatives. He does not get responsibilities as he is perceived as being too small to take one. He would also not be held responsible in a strict manner for mistakes that he would commit. It becomes a matter of habit for everybody to take it in their stride and not giving responsibilities to him. Finally the young child is left only to get love and affection in abundance.

With nothing to do and everybody standing on their toes to attend to his wishes does make one arrogant, demanding, selfish and self-centered. Usually such behavior makes one a misfit with others. The ones who are endowed with these traits are always under great stress.

The king baby syndrome "I want it and I want it now" is the thread of philosophy and attitude that the youngest one lives by. Anything going against it induces stress, anger, frustration and results into socially unacceptable behavior which is always self-destructive.

Often these frustrations are vented out in aggressive, withdrawn, uncooperative or irritable behavior. Sometimes the individual has befriended people with drug taking habits. The company of these friends (with drug taking behavior) results in channelizing all frustrations into drug taking. This gives immediate relief and also satisfies the reason to rebel.

Only son amongst daughters is another situation which compels parents and daughters alike to shower the individual with love, caring, affection and standing on their toes to attend to his little or big demands. If the individual happens to be the only son or the youngest of siblings amongst daughters then the above mentioned doling out of emotions magnifies manifold. The relatives too fall in line to shower love and affection on the individual.

Such individuals grow up with the habit of throwing tantrums and getting things their way. They build themselves into selfish, self – centered individuals who are only demanding things for themselves overlooking the needs of others and the prevailing circumstances in the family. They do not care for any body's interests and are disrespectful to others in the family. Their psyche is always at war with the world if their demands are not met or they are not shown due love and respect.

They are at war with themselves as they have very low frustration tolerance to things and situations that do not work their way all the time.

They are prone to look for attention and praise everywhere and fall prey to people who show "love" affection towards them. They are prone to follow suggestions from outsiders who can win their confidence easily by showing concern and love towards them. They are very easily swept into vices including drug taking.

They have dealt with their stresses in the past by demanding things which have to be fulfilled immediately. When they cannot handle the frustrations of their demands being rejected then Drugs give them immediate relief from their stresses.

Only daughter is also a much pampered soul. In the affluent class they are selfish, show-offs, self – centered and above all aggressive in their countenance. They too have been brought up with lot of care, tenderness, pampering and have got used to people attending to their wishes and whims.

They grow up into immature individuals who are very harsh on others and totally driven by focused fulfilling of their self needs thus providing satisfaction to themselves only and overlooking needs of others. They become very disrespectful to those whom they perceive as impediments towards their demand fulfillment.

These individuals are prone to fall prey to rebellious behavior as drug taking, getting into trouble with authorities and friends.

The middle order siblings do not get the same attention that the eldest or the youngest have got and responsibilities are also given to them. They grow up with feelings of discrimination that they feel in presence of the eldest or the youngest one. They are aware of the fact that they would not get what all they desire as easily as the eldest or the youngest. They do harbor feelings of resentment and jealousy towards the preferred siblings. The resentments soon build in their psyche as a prevailing mood of feeling neglected with low self-esteem. Some with these persistent feelings have developed persistent feelings of anxieties or sadness.

They often find it difficult to deal with these feelings. Thus they fall easy prey to addictions which offers them solace from these anxieties and also helps them belong to a group that cares for them.

Though the middle sibling is a major group in any family as they can be more than one and many but eldest and the youngest would always be one per family. Despite the fact that their proportion is large in a family compared to the eldest and the youngest their lot falling prey to addiction is proportionately low.

They have usually been under control of the elders in the family and the eldest sibling. They have had to compromise when their demands are always placed second to those of the preferred/pampered sibling, or second to the current household requirements. They have had to attend to many chores that the preferred ones have easily bye passed. Their actions have always been under scrutiny and they have not been given the freedom of the eldest or the pampered freedom of the youngest.

"You must give regard and respect and obey your elders" is one thing that is expected of the middle order siblings. "Your younger sibling is small and you must forego your interests for the sake of the younger one. You should take care of the younger one"

The middle order individual is bound between these norms and thus is more disciplined and has learnt to subdue his priorities for the sake of others.

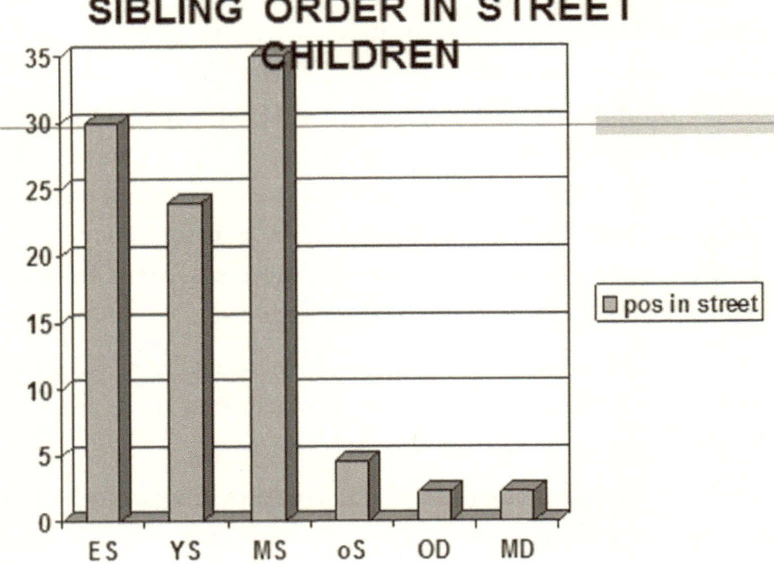

ES-Eldest Son, YS-Youngest Son, MS-Middle Son, OS-Only Son, OD-Only Daughter, MD-Middle Daughter

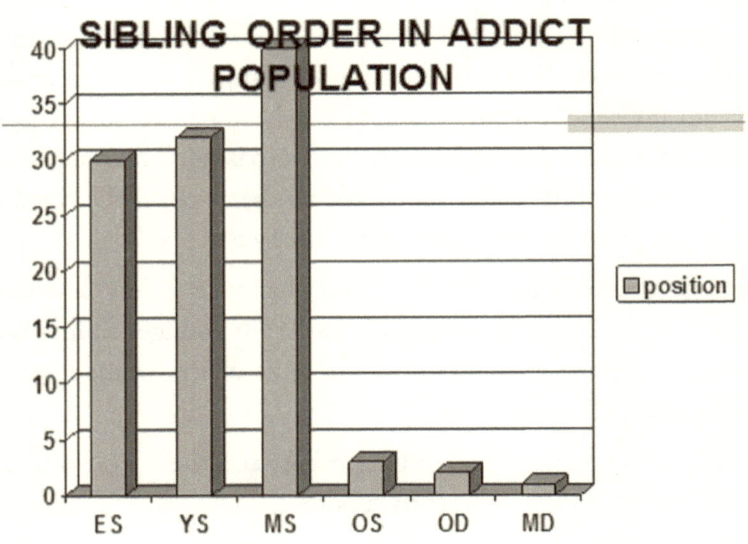

Figure showing sibling order in addict population. ES-Eldest Son, YS- Youngest Son, MS-Middle Son, OS- Only Son, OD- Only Daughter, MD-Middle Daughter

Dependence in Family

Dependence or addiction of any substance in a significant or even a non-significant family member happens to be the single most major factors responsible for vulnerability to addiction in other persons in the family. Addiction to any substance starts due to curiosity, experimentation and *modelling* after someone in the family who happens to be an addict.

The presence of an addict in the family is a constant exposure which gives rise to inquisitiveness, and desire to experiment in the tender minds of children, adolescents and young adults. The impressionable mind and the psyche of other individuals in a family may develop resentments towards the addict. The addict enjoys freedom of coming and going at will and absolutely no responsibility that he/she shoulders. In many homes the addict also gets to throw his/her tantrums and has the whole household on their knees. This is perceived as a power to control others. Such role models are present amongst addict friends and also in the society. Every society has individuals who are known alcoholics with very obnoxious behaviors and people are fearful of them.

Then there is also exposure to films which has been inadvertently glamorizing addiction just for the extra moolah that it earns. Actors are seen singing, dancing under influence of alcohol with beautiful girls. Girls too are depicted as being endearing and boisterous after consuming a shot of liquor. Youngsters get encouraged to live a life as they see it on the silver screen.

Though there are many films that depict addiction in its true colors but we want to see what is enjoyable and easily shy away from the realistic portrayal of addiction. Vices have been attractive for humans as far back as you can see in time.

In the present times the society has changed substantially. It has become a norm to celebrate any occasion with drinks, be it a birthday party, a reunion, a marriage or simply dining out. Alcohol has become accepted as a necessity often equated with being modern.

Here we are considering dependence in the family as a major factor responsible for drug addiction.

DEPENDENCE IN FAMILY

	Ethanol Dependence	Opiate Dependence	Cannabis Dependence
Street Children-	30%-F 4% -M	7.2%-F 4% -M	5%-F 2%-M
School Children-	13%-F	----	5%
Drug - Dependants	40%-F 2% -M	7.0% ---	5% ----

The table above shows the dependence to various drugs in the families of the population studied.

F=FATHER, M=MOTHER.

Dependence in Street Children Families

Besides an economic status that hangs on a shoe string budget we see an increased number of addiction cases in some other member of the families of street children which further add an economic, emotional and unhealthy burden on all individuals in the family.

- Alcohol dependence: 30 %(Thirty percent) of fathers approximately are heavily addicted to alcohol. Usually these are locally brewed varieties which are very cheap. The alcohol intake usually begins in the daytime and is there all the time round the clock.

  4% (Four percent) of mothers have been alcohol dependent in such families.

- Opiate dependence: 7.2 %(Seven point two percent) of fathers in street children families are addicted to opiates. The opiates have been opium, Dodda (opium husk)/smack or Dextro propoxyphene capsules. Brown sugar was the main stay addiction from 1980s to mid-2000. It was rampant as an epidemic and was easily available. It was not very expensive and could be purchased in the initial stages of addiction. Later on these individuals are unable to earn money and thus the finances start dwindling. However If one wants it one can beg, borrow or steal. As time went by it became impure with other things being mixed in it to increase its bulk and "kick". It became very dangerous to the body. There were many treatment programs as the number of addicts seeking treatment was ever increasing.

- 4 % (Four percent) of mothers from these families have been opiate abusers and this has usually been smack.

- Cannabis dependence: 5 %(Five percent) of fathers were abusing and were dependent on cannabis full time. Poly addiction was common in all these cases addicted to smack or cannabis.

- 2 %(Two percent) of mothers from the family of street children were dependent on cannabis.

- Besides the prevalence of addiction there is also the maladjusted behavior of addict parents which contributes to the pathological family milieu. The environment which is filled with aggression, cheating, lying, manipulations, stealing, police cases, hunger and poverty has all the essential soil to reap future addicts.

Dependence in School Children Families

These families are having a better background economically. However the addiction to any substance that runs in these families is detailed below. This data represents a private school population analysis.

Alcohol dependence: 13 %(Thirteen percent) of fathers from school children families had *alcohol addiction* problems. This seems very low given the fact that alcohol has now a social sanction of sorts and is a part of all types of celebrations. Thus even though we may have social drinkers in many families but they are below danger mark as yet because alcohol has not become a problem drinking for them. They have as yet not become ALCOHOLICS.

Incidentally rarely any mother reported with an alcohol problem. Now there is a noticeable trend of accepting alcohol by ladies in social circles. This contributes to women facing alcohol dependence problems.

- Opiate dependence: incidentally none of the parents reported with any opiate dependence amongst school going children who were dependent on inhalants.

- Cannabis dependence: 5 %(Five percent) of fathers had dependence to cannabis.

Mothers did not report with cannabis dependence problem.

Dependence in Drug Addict Families

These families display pre-existing addictions in the parents. Thus exposure to an environment where someone is getting intoxicated frequently and exhibiting an inebriated state with brash talk and related abnormal behavior is a consistent feature in such families. This is something a growing child (the future addict) witnesses from a very young age daily in his life.

Additionally these families have a whole lot of maladaptive behavior patterns to be seen. Disturbed parent's relationship, violence, abusiveness, and lying, high tension emotional dramas and cheating. Financial crisis and problems that go with it are further contributing to an already unstable, unhealthy atmosphere. Usually an addict's family has economic stresses which could be either the cause or effect of addiction.

History of addiction in parents is detailed here.

- Alcohol dependence: 40 % (Forty percent) of fathers of addict families are alcoholics in its florid form. This contributes to a family getting a disturbed or disrupted environment.

  2 %(Two percent) of the mothers in addict families has alcohol dependence.

- Opiate dependence: 7 % (Seven percent) of fathers were dependent on opiates. Usually brown sugar or dextro-propoxyphene capsules.

  Mothers did not report any dependence to opiates.

- Cannabis dependence: 5 % (Five percent) of fathers of families that reared children into future addicts had dependence to cannabis.

Mothers in these families did not report such dependence.

Violence in Families

The family in which there is a drug or alcohol problem with a member is characterized by violence either in words or actions. Either the violence is directed against one individual or all members. Often when children are small they are mute spectators to these disturbing scenes or they simply walk out of the house as is seen with street children.

We studied the prevalence of violence in the families of our patients. The results are mentioned below.

- *Street children*: 92 % (Ninety two percent) of the street children had suffered aggressive, violent behavior from parents or surrogates. They reported regular beatings which had been slaps, kicks, boxes, or even getting flogged with belts.

- Abusing was a consistent part of all interactions within the family where the addicted member would curse and abuse one or all members.

  Often the parents would resort to stop food of the child being beaten up. The pretexts for beatings had been trivial to negligible. Stopping food is another form of violence the addict faces when he has to go to bed empty stomach.

- *School children*: 10 % (Ten percent) of school going children had witnessed violence at the hands of an addict parent. These were not consistent and of very low ferocity. The aim of such beatings was not to harm the child but definitely to discipline him. The addict parent has lost all patience in the course of his addiction history. He cannot reasonably discuss any problems at home in a friendly manner with his children.

- The child could also invite wrath of the addict parent if he was rebelling against him/her. That outcome could be seriously harmful. The child would get beaten up more aggressively on the pretext of disciplining him. His pocket allowance stopped and other privileges taken away.

- *Drug addicts*: 32 %(Thirty two percent) had experienced regular violence at home. It was usually the father who was abusive and violent. The targets were usually the mother but it could be anybody in the family who did not conform to the addict father's wishes or rebelled against him. In such situations the violence was proportionately greater.

- The shades of violence include abusing, beating with bare hands, kicking or using objects as stick, bat, breaking things, turning a member out of the house, and shouting.

VARIOUS INHALANTS ABUSED AND THEIR PERCENTAGE

The table below highlights the abuse of various inhalants percentage wise.

VARIOUS INHALANTS ABUSED	
▪ TYPEWRITER FLUID	---------------------------------55 %
▪ ADHESIVE	-------------------------------12 %
▪ PETROL	--------------------------------17 %
▪ THINNER/VARNISH	-------------------------------6 %
▪ GLUE	-----------------------------2 %
▪ CAR EXHAUST FUMES	-------------------------------2 %
▪ CAMPHOR	------------------------------1 %
▪ NAPHTHALENE	-------------------------------2 %
▪ RUBEFACIENTS	------------------------------1 %
▪ BUTANE- (CFC) –NOT USED	
▪ PHENYL, VASELINE, ANTISEPTIC	-------------------------------1 %
▪ CARBORIZED MATCHSTICKS	
▪ BURNING TYRES	------------------------------1 %

Typewriter Fluid

This tops the list of popularity amongst inhalants with nearly 55 % (fifty five percent) of inhalant abusers using it. This seems to be very popular amongst all classes whether rich or poor, educated or illiterate, boys or girls. It is in demand with street children just as much as it is with dependent office going inhalant abusers.

The main ingredient of the typewriter fluid is Toluene which acts as a central nervous system depressant and on sniffing deeply gives a high.

Essentially there are two types of typewriter fluids very neatly packed in two bottles. One is called the *whitener* and the other called the *correction fluid*. These are spill proof packing and very cheap. Very convenient to carry in your bag or pockets, or lady bags.

Both the fluids have been used as inhalants by simply putting a few drops on a piece of cloth and inhaling deeply at regular intervals till one gets a high.

Typewriter Fluid

The Whitener and the Correction fluid both come as two separate bottles but packed in a single unit box.

Tuck-T Adhesive

This is an adhesive which comes in tubes. A jelly like consistency and used as a medium to stick two rubber pieces together. Used by bicycle mechanics to mend punctures in cycle tyre tubes.

Cheap and very easily available. It's called "solution" in street language. Again it is simply put on a piece of cloth and inhaled regularly by taking deep breaths. First deep breaths are for the high and later ones are to maintain the high.

The ingredients are Toluene, Chlorinated solvents as Methyl Chloride, Methyl Ethyl Chloride.

It is the next commonly used inhalant and it is used mainly by street children. Twelve percent (12 %) of street children have a preference for this over typewriter fluid.

Petrol

This is also a preferred inhalant for abuse by street children. 17 %(Seventeen percent) of the street children feed their addiction by procuring petrol. They usually do so by stealing from cars, garages.

Petrol is emptied in small amounts into a small container. The vapors released are inhaled by "huffing" from the mouth of the container after opening the lid of the container.

Often the petrol is poured in small amounts in a polythene bag and vapors huffed repeatedly.

Petrol could also be poured into a small sized bottle/metallic box with a piece of cloth dipped and soaked in it. The vapor is now "puffed" by encircling the cloth with the palm in a firm grip and then inhaling by puffing with the mouth at the soaked cloth.

The active ingredients are Hexane, Septane, Octane, Cyclic Aromatic Hydro carbons.

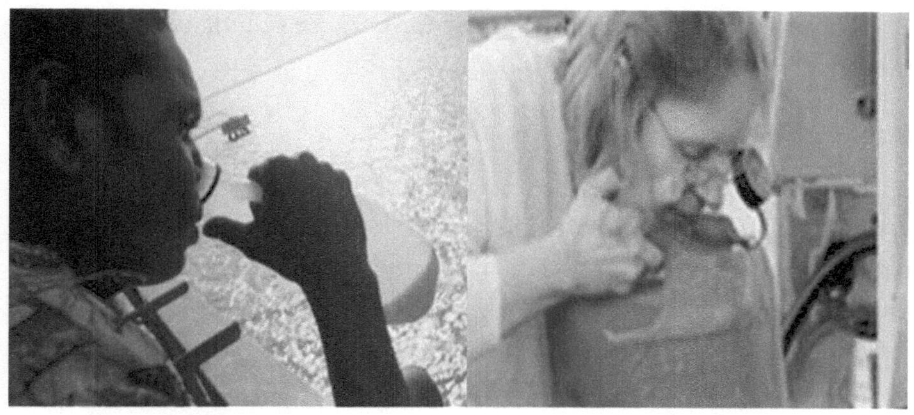

Huffing Petrol Vapors   *Sniffing Petrol Vapors*

Varnish and Thinners

For Six percent (6 %) street children the preferred inhalant of abuse is varnish and thinners. These are organic solvents used in painting wooden furniture and many other items. They are in liquid form and the active ingredient in these is Toluene, Acetone, Methylene Chloride and Petroleum distillates.

Essentially these are abused by sniffing, huffing, and or puffing.

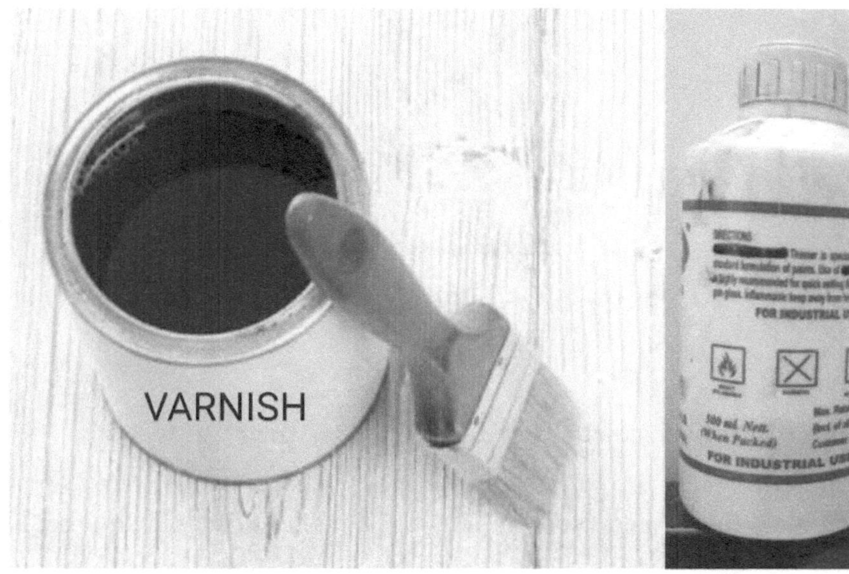

Varnish   *Thinner*

The way they are put in containers for purpose of inhaling is similar to modes of using as mentioned under petrol abuse.

Nail Polish Remover

Many nail polish removers contain acetone, a chemical solvent that is very effective as a paint thinner, industrial cleanser and solvent. This clear, colorless liquid belongs to a class of chemicals called ketones. Ketones are produced as a byproduct of human metabolism, but they are also synthesized for industrial purposes.

Abused by girls who have easier access to it as part of their vanity kits. Nail polish remover can be inhaled directly from the bottle, poured into a bag and inhaled by mouth, or sniffed from a rag (piece of cloth) that has been soaked in the nail polish remover.

Nail Polish Remover

Glue

An adhesive substance used for sticking objects or materials together.

Synthetic glues are made of polyvinyl acetate (PVA) emulsions. Emulsion is a fine dispersion of minute droplets of one liquid in another in which it is not soluble or miscible. The word emulsion refers to the fact that the PVA particles have been emulsified or suspended in water. In addition to water and PVA, synthetic glue can also contain ingredients like ethanol, acetone, and amyl acetate. Ethanol slows down the drying time, acetone speeds up the drying time, and amyl acetate slows down the evaporation of the glue.

The glue is spread on a piece of cloth and sniffed regularly to get a high and sustain it. Two percent of inhalant abusers (2%) are glue sniffers. It has been my experience that mostly it is seen amongst street children, carpenters.

Teenagers in school going age groups use it as well for getting a high especially for the ease with which it can be carried along undetected.

Naphthalene Balls

Naphthalene Mothballs are small balls of chemical pesticide and deodorant, sometimes used when storing clothing and other articles susceptible to damage from mold or moth larvae.

Naphthalene is made from crude oil or coal tar. It is also produced when things burn, so naphthalene is found in cigarette smoke, car exhaust, and smoke from forest fires. Naphthalene is an organic compound with formula $C_{10}H_8$. It is the simplest polycyclic aromatic hydrocarbon, and is a white crystalline solid with a characteristic odor. It is used as an insecticide and pest repellent.

Mothballs are a pesticide product that contains either naphthalene or Para dichlorobenzene as active ingredients. Both of these chemicals are toxic fumigants (which mean they volatilize into the air) and must be present in high concentrations to be effective.

The naphthalene balls are crushed and placed in a handkerchief and the vapors are then inhaled. It is often crushed and rubbed vigorously between the palms to be inhaled regularly from the palm which is closed lightly into a fist. The vapors are puffed from the thumb side of loosely closed fist.

Naphthalene Balls

Two percent (2%) of inhalant abusers have a strong choice for naphthalene balls. Mostly these are street children. School going teens are not abusing naphthalene or moth balls.

Car Exhaust Fumes

One wonders why people inhale car exhaust fumes for a high. But there is always a way in any madness. Experimenting with the fact that if petrol or diesel can be intoxicating why not the exhaust fumes emitted by diesel or petrol vehicles. To add to this is the desperation to try out anything. And above all in this case one does not require carrying anything he has just to be where a car engine is running and emitting exhaust fumes.

Nearly 2 %(Two percent) of street children are addicted to car fumes.

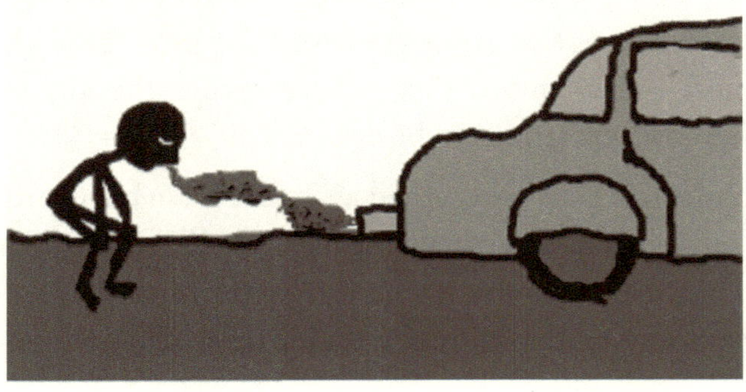

Man Inhaling Car Exhaust Fumes

The smoke emitted from motor vehicles has many poisonous gases. These are as listed below:

- Hydrocarbons (HC)
- Nitrogen oxides (NOx)
- Carbon monoxide (CO)
- Sulfur dioxide (SO2)
- Hazardous air pollutants (toxics)
- Greenhouse gases.
- Particulate matter (PM). These particles of soot and metals give smog its murky color.

A light headedness due to suffocation can be caused by the mere physical consistency of the smoke. One feels choked when exposed for an uncomfortable period to such fumes. If the fumes are dense say at a congested traffic signal then one cannot stand it for more than 10 to 15 seconds.

The chemicals that are emitted have a profound effect on the nervous system and hence give the high which often turns out to be lethal.

John Scott Haldane's experiment on himself with carbon monoxide gas demonstrates the effects and lethal effects. This has been discussed under pathophysiology.

Carbon monoxide mainly causes adverse effects by combining with hemoglobin to form carboxyhemoglobin (HbCO) in the blood. This prevents hemoglobin from carrying oxygen to the tissues.

Phenyl

Synonyms include carbolic acid, hydroxybenzene, monohydroxybenzene, benzenol, mono phenol, phenyl hydroxide, phenyl alcohol, phenic acid, phenylic acid, and phenylic alcohol.

Persons exposed only to phenol vapor do not pose substantial risks of secondary contamination. Persons whose clothing or

Phenyl

skin is contaminated with liquid phenol can secondarily contaminate other personnel by direct contact or through off-gassing vapor. Their clothes let out vapors which intoxicate those in near proximity.

Phenol is a flammable, highly corrosive chemical with a sickeningly sweet, acrid odor. Phenol's odor generally provides adequate warning of hazardous concentrations.

Phenol is well absorbed by all routes of exposure. Exposure by any route can cause systemic effects which are intoxication in mild doses and fatal at higher doses.

Inhaled after putting on a piece of cloth or directly from the bottle.

Nearly 1 %(one percent) of inhalant abusers take a fancy to Phenyl to get their high. It is seen amongst street children mainly.

Antiseptic

The active ingredient that confers its antiseptic property is chloroxylenol (C_8H_9ClO), an aromatic chemical compound. Chloroxylenol comprises 4.8% of Dettol's total admixture, with the rest made up by pine oil, isopropanol, castor oil, soap and water.

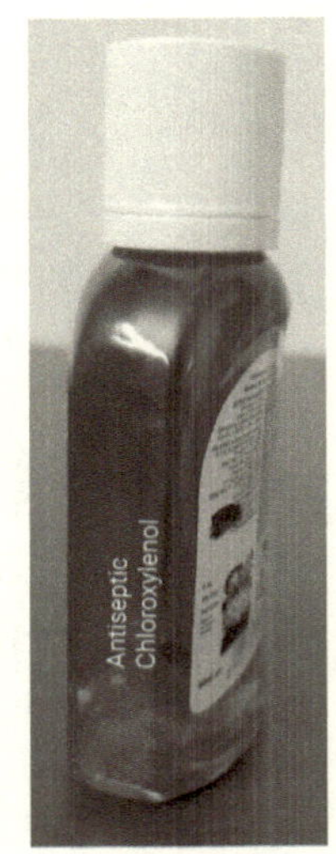

Antiseptic

It is poured on a piece of cloth which is then placed between the palms and then the vapors are inhaled vigorously.

One percent (1 %) of inhalant abusers have a preference for chloroxylenol only often as a filler when they do not get their inhalant of first choice.

It is rare to be hooked onto only antiseptic solution and stay with it. As time passes the preference to this is given up as more convenient options come up. Options that are easier to carry and do not get noticed by their smell. Dettol has an unmistakable smell and is easily noticed by one and all.

Soft Paraffin

Petroleum jelly/petrolatum/white petrolatum/soft paraffin/paraffin wax or multi-hydrocarbon (mixture of many hydrocarbons with carbon numbers mainly higher than 25), originally promoted as a topical ointment for its healing properties. The soft paraffin is kept in alcohol base to give it the right consistency and properties that make it a cosmetic necessity.

After petroleum jelly became a medicine chest staple, consumers began to use it for many ailments as well as cosmetic purposes, including toenail fungus, genital rashes (non-STD), nosebleeds, diaper rash, and chest colds. Its folkloric medicinal value as a "cure-all" has since been limited by better scientific understanding of appropriate and inappropriate uses. It is recognized by the U.S. Food and Drug Administration (FDA) as an approved over-the-counter (OTC) skin protectant, and remains widely used in cosmetic skin care. In India too it is used for skin protection, and cosmetic care.

The Paraffin jelly is placed in a piece of cloth and inhaled or sniffed to get a high.

About less than 1 %(one percent) of inhalant abusers take Vaseline. The street children are more frequent users. It is negligible in other people.

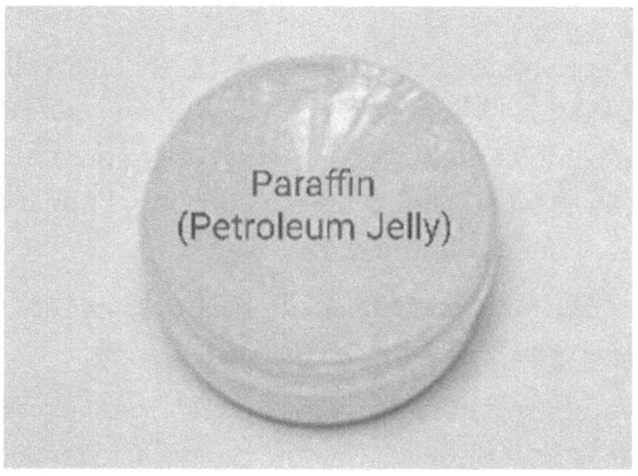

Paraffin Lotion

Rubefacient

A rubefacient is a substance for topical application that produces redness of the skin e.g. by causing dilation of the capillaries and an increase in blood circulation. It is used for reducing acute or chronic pain.

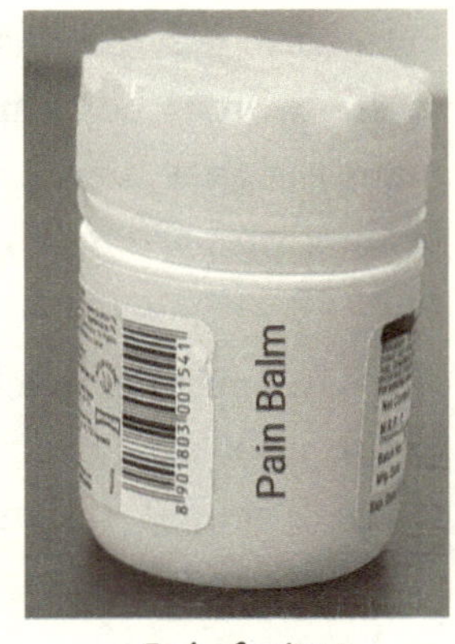

Rubefacient

A scented rubefacient that has been used for more than one and a quarter centuries in India.it was produced first time in 1893. It's very popular for alleviating headaches, back pain, sprains by being applied topically on the skin above the painful area. It is a household "must have". It is Amrutanjan and has been steadfastly holding its credibility as a pain reliever.

Strong Pain Balm

Active Ingredient/Active Moiety

MENTHOL (MENTHOL)	MENTHOL	0.15 g in 1 g
METHYL SALICYLATE (SALICYLIC ACID)	METHYL SALICYLATE	0.15 g in 1 g

Another rubifacient is essentially made of Gandepura oil (Wintergreen oil), Nilgiri oil, Pudina (Mint) flower, Laung (Clove) oil, Turpentine oil in a proportionate combination (20g Contains: Gandapuro oil (Wintergreen Oil) 4%, Turpentine oil 800 mg, Nilgiri oil 800 mg, Pudina flower 600 mg, Lavang oil 20 mg, In An Ointment Base Q.S).

Tragically it has also found popularity with inhalant abusers who would sniff it by applying it on their palms or on a piece of cloth.

Another way of consuming amongst some inhalant abusers is absolutely out of the world and simply beats your imagination. I wonder if considering this mode of intake would give us a need to categorize them as a special class of abusers.

The rubefacient is spread over a piece of bread and then placed in a refrigerator (in the freezer compartment) for some time say half an hour. It is then taken out and eaten to get a high.

Less than 1 % of inhalant abusers consume the rubefacients that are mentioned above. It is also not a drug of choice. It is used as filler, a substitute when the preferred addiction is not available.

Camphor

Camphor is a waxy, flammable, white or transparent solid with a strong aroma. It is a terpenoid with the chemical formula C10H16O

It is found in the wood of the camphor laurel (Cinnamomum camphora), a large evergreen tree found in Asia (particularly in Sumatra, Indonesia and Borneo) and also in the wood of the unrelated "Kapur tree" (Dryobalanops aromatic) a tall timber tree from the same region. A major source of camphor in Asia is camphor basil (the parent of African blue basil). Camphor can also be synthetically produced from oil of turpentine. It is used for its scent, as an ingredient in cooking (mainly in India), as an embalming fluid, for medicinal purposes, and in religious ceremonies.

I am very sure its intoxicating value must have been discovered due to the pursuit of an addict to find newer inhalants. We could say with certainty the inhalant abuser are always sniffing at various goods as a reflex, with an idea to experiment. And it may have been the inquisitive nosing around with camphor that revealed its intoxicating properties.

It is rubbed between the palms and or simply kept in the hand with palm closed and sniffed time and again for the high. Some inhalant abusers mainly street children chew it as well. How chewing works to get a high is simply farfetched. I believe the consistency and the vapors mixed with saliva may be another sensation that one is hooked to.

Less than 1 %(one percent) of inhalant abusers are using it. It is always a "time pass", a substitute or just as an add-on to an already high individual. It does not present ever as a primary or preferred intoxicant.

Camphor Tablets

Miscellaneous Inhalants of Abuse

In India the other forms of inhalants of abuse would include

- Inhaling burning rubber tyres smoke. Resorted to by the street urchins. The fire releases a dark, thick smoke that contains cyanide, carbon monoxide, sulfur dioxide, and products of butadiene and styrene. Again it's the carbon monoxide which gives the high. These are poisonous gases and have a fatal effect if the smoke is in a closed area.

The other very rare anecdotal forms of inhalant abuse are-

- Inhaling burning match sticks smoke. This too releases gases as sulphur dioxide, carbon dioxide. The smoke has an aroma to which the addict is hooked and nothing more to it.

- Inhaling crackers smoke-Firecrackers contain elements like copper, cadmium, sulphur, aluminum, barium and many such more elements which give the vibrant colors after the crackers burn. The smoke released contains suspended impurities which have a very disastrous effect on health.

CLINICAL PRESENTATION

SIGNS AND SYMPTOMS OF INHALANT ABUSE

- Chemical smell or odor on breath or body
- Redness, sores, or spots around the lips or mouth
- Redness of eyes
- Running or red nose
- Paint stains on clothing or body
- Nausea or loss of appetite
- Drunken or dazed appearance
- Dizziness
- Irritability, excitability, or anxiety
- Slow verbal responses in conversation
- Sudden behavior change
- Sensitivity to light
- Sore or irritated throat
- Rashes or redness on hands
- Organic brain syndrome (i.e., coarse tremor, staggering gait, speech problems, thought disorder)
- Decreased attention span, intoxication, mood disorder, dementia, impulsivity, decreased attention, and withdrawal.
- Decreased intelligence quotient.

SIGNS OF INHALANT INTOXICATION

Recent intentional use or short-term high-dose exposure to volatile inhalants results in a clinically characteristic clinical signs that developed during or shortly after use of volatile inhalants.

The signs are as follows:

- Dizziness
- Nystagmus
- Incoordination in motor activity
- Slurred speech
- Unsteady gait
- Lethargy
- Depressed reflexes
- Psychomotor retardation – slowness in mentation, speech and physical activity.
- Tremor
- Generalized muscle weakness
- Blurred vision or diplopia
- Stupor or coma
- Euphoria

Confused State

A confused state is a common presentation amongst inhalant abusers. This is because the inhalant abusers are seldom aware about the dose that they are consuming. With each inhalation the need for the next one gets more pronounced and with the individuals repeated inhalations the dose becomes excess and cognition gets compromised.

INHALANT INDUCED MEDICAL CONDITIONS

INHALANT INDUCED DELIRIUM

In overdosing the individual would eventually get delirious. Inhalant intoxication delirium is due to overdose of inhalants in a short time. The delirium is characterized by the following signs and symptoms.

- Disturbance of consciousness.
- Reduced ability to focus, sustain, or shift attention.
- Altered behavior as irritability, agitation, violence.
- Irrelevant speech, slurring of speech.
- Disorientation.
- Illusions.
- Hallucinations.
- Tremors
- Fluctuating levels of consciousness.

Disturbance occurs over a short period and tends to fluctuate during the course of the day. Thus the confusion and agitation seem to wax and wane in inhalant induced delirium.

The clinician must exclude symptoms of delirium due to other known preexisting, established causes involving the central nervous system and dementia that may have set in the course of inhalant abuse. This is done by taking a detailed personal history, family history and referring to investigations done in the past and present. Additional investigations may be required to support his clinical findings.

Some medications used in various specialties are known to cause a side effect of delirium. The list of all such commonly used medications can be referred to in Appendix 1.

Some of these medications are commonly abused along with inhalants as they are easily available. Thus antihistamines in cough syrups, tonics containing alcohol, the sedative hypnotics (sleeping pills in poly drug abuse) are to be looked for if delirium is being evaluated.

INHALANT INDUCED PERSISTENT DEMENTIA

Long term use of inhalants results in wide spread damage to the brain tissues and the spinal cord leading to a wide range of neurological and cognitive symptoms. There is a loss of the covering layer of the neuron (nerve cell) in large areas of the brain and spinal cord. The brain shrinks in size in the cortex, and the cerebellum. There is white cell degeneration as we call it and the resulting dementia is White Matter Dementia. This has been highlighted in the past chapters. The brain functions are compromised in memory, orientation and cognitive functions during intoxication with inhalants and these deficits carry on even after the inhalant effect wears off in chronic users.

Few inhalant dependents have been studied prospectively. Despite some reports of improvement after abstention most neurocognitive deficits persist and worsen. Additionally as neurocognitive deficits advance to dementia the inhalant dependent individual loses the cognitive capacity to avoid relapses and each relapse advances the brain degeneration.

Development of multiple cognitive deficits manifested in both domains as mentioned below-

1.   Memory Impairment

Broadly speaking the three types of memory are the immediate, recent and remote. These are impaired as the disease progresses. In chronic abuser these memory functions are impaired and functioning is compromised

Immediate Memory

These are memory for events or information in the last few hours or days. Brain damage that limits one's ability to store new information may impair immediate memory but have no effect on memories of the distant past.

Immediate memory impairment affects the working of the individual in the current time. There is a tendency to forget what has transpired in the present context and a linear association of events is not there. The action that one takes in this situation thus gets inappropriate.

This impairment makes the inhalant abuser unable to retain and recall most of what happens presently. In a matter of a day or two the memory fades away with no or very little recollection of what all transpired.

Recent Memory

Short-term memory. Also called working memory.

Recent memory is a system for temporarily storing and managing the information required to carry out complex cognitive tasks such as learning, reasoning, and comprehension. Recent memory is involved in the selection, initiation, and termination of information-processing functions such as encoding, storing, and retrieving data.

Inhalant abuse results in damage to brain areas responsible for recent memory.

Remote Memory

Long-term memory is that aspect of memory in which knowledge is stored permanently, to be activated when cued; it is theoretically unlimited in capacity. Recent memory the ability to recall events from the immediate past. Remote memory the ability to recall events from the distant past.

Remote memory is stored in a different area in the brain. The storage of immediate and recent memory is in other different areas of the brain.

Remote memories is intact in the initial stages of inhalant abuse but later with chronic abuse of inhalants these too get impaired and lost.

2.   Impairment of Cognitive Executive Functions

Executive function is a set of mental skills that help you get things done. These skills are controlled by an area of the brain called the frontal lobe. Executive functions include basic cognitive processes such as attentional control, cognitive inhibition, inhibitory control, working memory, and cognitive flexibility. Cognitive control is impaired in addiction, attention deficit hyperactivity disorder, autism, and a number of other central nervous system disorders.

The other deficits that could be due to inhalant damage to the brain are-

Aphasia – Aphasia is *an inability to comprehend and formulate language* because of damage to specific brain regions due to inhalant abuse over a long period. Other causes are cerebrovascular accidents, head injury, infections of the brain, exposure to toxic substances.

Apraxia – The *inability to execute a voluntary motor movement* despite being able to demonstrate normal muscle function. Apraxia is not related to a lack of understanding or to any kind of physical paralysis; rather, it is caused by damage in the cortex of the brain. Specifically it is the posterior parietal cortex which is involved.

Apraxia of speech (AOS) is an acquired oral motor speech disorder affecting an individual's ability to translate conscious speech plans into spoken speech, which results in limited and difficult speech ability. Individuals with AOS have difficulty connecting speech messages from the brain to the mouth. With apraxia of speech a person finds it difficult or impossible to move his or her mouth and tongue to speak. This happens, even though the person has the desire to speak the mouth and tongue muscles are physically unable to form words.

Agnosia – This is an *inability to process sensory inputs such as light, sound, and touch.* Agnosia is typically a result of brain injury. For example, damaging the back part of the brain can cause visual agnosia (inability to properly recognize objects by sight).

Often there is a loss of ability to recognize objects, persons, sounds, shapes, or smells while the specific sense is not defective nor is there any significant memory loss.

Disturbance in executive functions can cause significant impairment in social or occupational functioning and represents a major decline from a previous level of functioning.

Evidence comes from history, physical examination, or laboratory findings, radiological findings that deficits are etiologically related to the persistent effects of substance use.

OTHER CONDITIONS

Inhalant Induced Anxiety Disorders

The disorder is characterized by anxiety or fear, sometimes accompanied by such physical symptoms as racing heart, breathless and shakiness, caused by the effects of a psychoactive substance. Although "anxiety" and "fear" are often used interchangeably, the former term generally means an unpleasant emotional state for which the cause is not apparent or which is perceived to be uncontrollable, while the latter is usually the emotional and physical response to an identifiable threat. It has been said that anxiety is the anticipation of future events, while fear is a reaction to current events.

These symptoms may occur while the patient is under the influence of the drug (intoxication) or after use of the drug has stopped (withdrawal). Generalized anxiety, panic attacks or manifestations of phobia may be precipitated by inhalant use or withdrawal.

Anxiety caused by the drug may persist as long as use continues, while withdrawal-related symptoms may first manifest themselves up to four weeks after cessation of use (Galanter and Kleber, 2008).

Inhalant Induced Obsessions and Compulsions

OCD or Obsessive Compulsive Disorder could be seen during inhalant abuse or during withdrawal from inhalants.

Inhalant Induced Mood Disorders

Though rare it is seen in individuals who are predisposed to mood disorders, and who are using inhalants. Other drugs especially cannabis and alcohol are known to precipitate Hypomanic or Manic states in predisposed individuals.

Inhalant Induced Psychotic Disorders

Frank psychotic symptoms as persecutory delusions, hallucinations and resulting abnormal behavior have been seen with chronic inhalant abuse. The abnormal behavior results in suspiciousness towards people, withdrawn, avoidant behavior or conversely aggressive behavior. This can result in self-harming or harming others and therefore is a medical/psychiatric emergency.

DIAGNOSIS OF INHALANT ABUSE

The clinicians has to take a thorough history as often the inhalant abusers are likely to be missed in very early stages of addiction. History taking carefully and systematically uncovers changes in behavior, changes in eating and sleeping habits, change of friends and friend circle, rise in daily expenses, and fall in scholastic performance as is reflected in the school report cards.

One should take into consideration the information given to parents of the addict by his close friends and acquaintances as well. This information is very vital and usually highlights the total time that the addict spends on addiction thus compromising other important activities. It also gives details of friends who are in the drug taking cliché.

The presentation of Inhalant abusers has its unmistakable characteristics which have been mentioned in the previous chapter/pages. These clinch the diagnosis for inhalant abuse except maybe nitrous oxide inhalation which does not have any chemical odor so characteristic of organic solvents. Nitrous oxide abuse is characterized by confused euphoric states and changes in behavior pattern which are noticed by the relatives.

Additionally the clinical examination elicits other signs related to Central Nervous System (hearing loss, headaches, cerebellar signs, paresis, motor impairment, Parkinsonism, encephalopathy).

Chest auscultation reveals rhonchi, crepitation, or evidence of pneumonitis.

Cardio Vascular System evaluation reveals a persistent tachycardia often with disturbed cardiac rhythm.

Muscular system which is affected by inhalant abuse is assessed for power, co-ordination, reflexes, tone and nutrition. These are impaired and have been discussed in previous chapters.

Mental status examination shows:

Appearance is one of a shabby, malnourished, unkempt individual who presents with a careless countenance.

The clients have smell of chemicals on their person and clothing.

There are stains around the lips or nostrils.

Attention and Concentration - There is usually difficulty in focusing Attention and sustaining it. The concentration is very transient and the patient gets distracted easily. Long term users look confused in the interview situations.

Orientation and Memory - Often the patient has confusion about dates and days.

Attitude - The client has difficulty comprehending questions. There is avoidance tactics for the interview. Often the patient is visibly irritated by the interview.

Mood variations are noticeable with joyfulness interspersed with irritability.

Higher Functions - Often inhalant abusers present with psychotic symptoms (usually chronic abusers).The patient could present with persecutory ideas that people are trying to harm him. He could be having ideas that people known and even strangers are making fun of him or passing comments on him. The client could also report hearing voices (auditory hallucinations) or seeing shadows, or people when there are none (visual hallucinations).

Judgment is affected as is reflected when pre-set questions are asked to assess his ability to evaluate and decide.

General knowledge is affected for current affairs and in chronic users it is very poor

Mathematical ability is affected as the patient can't focus on any subject. Thus simple calculations fail him as serial subtraction of 100-7, and also simple multiplications as 5.75 x 3

Biological Drives

- *Appetite*-There is a decline in food intake and reportedly the patient has lost significant weight in the past period from the onset of addiction to inhalants.

- *Sleep*- The sleep cycle is grossly disturbed with no specific pattern of sleeping.

Diagnostic Considerations

Substance-induced psychiatric disorders resemble the primary mental disorders as

- *Major depression*

- *Anxiety disorder*

- *Psychosis*

The above should be considered in the differential diagnosis and excluded as a primary affliction.

These are usually present as a cause or as an effect of inhalant intake.

A person with a personality disorder has a tendency to take care of his immediate anxieties by dousing them with some addiction or the other. The disorders to be excluded are-

- Conduct disorder

- Antisocial personality disorder

- Delinquency

Other conditions to be ruled out as primary conditions, where inhalant abuse has developed later on are-

- Alcohol abuse and dependence

- Cannabis abuse and dependence

- Temporal lobe epilepsy

- Poly substance dependence

- Physical and sexual abuse

WORKUP (INVESTIGATIONS)

Having come thus far we now go for specific laboratory investigations and radiological tests

Laboratory Studies that are prescribed and need to be done are:

1. Complete blood cell count with differential count and platelet count.

2. Sequential multiple analysis: It is the biochemical examination of various substances in the blood, such as albumin, alkaline phosphatase, bilirubin, calcium, and cholesterol, using a computerized laboratory analyzer that produces a printout showing measured values of the substances tested.

3. *Hippuric acid* concentration in the urine.

4. Electrolyte (e.g., sodium, potassium, chloride) levels. Electrolyte imbalance develops in inhalant abusers.

5. Anion Gap Measurement

6. Liver function tests

7. Kidney function tests

8. BUN (blood urea nitrogen) determination

9. Serum Creatinine level

10. Lipid profile

11. Urinalysis, with routine screenings for hippuric acid

12. Urine drug screen

13. Urine pregnancy test – there is an uninhibited sexual venture which leads to unwanted pregnancy.

14. 24- Hour urine test

15. Tests for sexually transmitted diseases

16. Rapid HIV test

17. HIV-antigen test

18. Thyrotropin testing

19. Thyroid function tests

20. Heavy metal screening test

Imaging Studies

Computerized Tomographic Scan - Order a Computerized Tomographic Scan if neurological symptoms are present (e.g., hearing loss, headaches, cerebellar signs, paresis, motor impairment, Parkinsonism, encephalopathy).

Electroencephalography - Perform an Electro-Encephalography to help identify seizure activity, specifically temporal lobe epilepsy.

Positron Emission Tomography - A positron emission tomography (PET) scan is desirable, if it is not feasible order a single-photon emission computed tomography scan to help identify nonhomogeneous uptake of radiopharmaceuticals, which may indicate areas of hypo function and hyper function of the brain.

A hospital care with all the modern sensitive tests as PET scan, MRI Scan, Blood analysis and many more is not accessible to all, specially the deprived poor of the society. Thus aim is to run a medical unit which can diagnose and treat adequately most inhalant abusers.

We have to make do within our means. At our center we used basic tests for all patients and referred others for higher investigations to higher centers. The essential basic laboratory tests I am referring to are

- Routine blood tests- Hemoglobin, TLC, DLC, ESR, Platelets, Liver Function Test, Kidney Function Test to assess kidney status.

- However the necessary tests have never been bypassed or ignored even if it means a monetary burden. Often the tests have been done complimentary.

- Serum electrolyte levels – serum sodium, potassium, chloride, calcium.

- Thyroid function tests

- Urine analysis routine and microscopic or further for culture and sensitivity if infection is present.

The radiological tests that we got done were

- X-ray Chest P-A view.

- MRI scan is advisable but can't be done in small budget centers. So for this referral to other centers were sought.

These tests give us substantial information on patient's health and also indications if further tests are required.

NEURO-PSYCHOLOGICAL TESTING

There are many tests available in our armamentarium. Routinely tests done are:

- Test to evaluate Intelligence Quotient (I.Q)

- Tests to evaluate Neurosis versus Psychosis (Rorschach Test)

- Tests to evaluate Emotional life of individual (Thematic Apperception Test)

- Tests to rule out Organic Brain damage (Bender Gestalt test)

The above mentioned tests identify many personality traits, abnormalities, psychiatric illnesses, and brain damage and serve also to decide future course of treatment. They consume time and money.

We in our practice took help of a relatively "no cost" test. Draw a Person test (DAPT) as it is called. This is easy to administer and can evaluate many parameters as I.Q, Neurosis, Psychosis, Organic Brain Damage.

Draw a Person Test

We have used it extensively and we found that it has a value of a very sensitive test which picks up latent psychiatric conditions and brain damage in the very early stages of inhalant abuse history. It is also a test which could be considered suited for hospitals running on low budget.

It is quite imperative that DAPT cannot replace the radiological tests and even the other psychological tests mentioned above. The interpretations of DAPT does save time, money and gives very clear indications about neurosis, psychosis, organic brain damage even before they show up on other tests or behavior.

There are very subtle changes that show up on the DAPT much earlier in the course of the illness and these changes in the drawing are obviously worsened with passing time.

I have compared the drawings of inhalant abusers from our clinic with the drawings of the normal children from school programs and one can see the typical abnormal characteristics in the drawings of inhalant abusers. Also as age advances we see gradual worsening of the DAPT drawings in the inhalant abusers indicating a further decline of brain functions, whereas with normal school children we see resolution of the immature drawings with a shift towards a normal drawing as age advances.

Organic Brain Disease

With inhalant abuse cortical damage is obvious in the MRI findings of the head much later in the course of the disease and usually when the patient starts showing behavioral abnormalities. Earlier changes are missed by parents/attendants and are wrongly interpreted as symptoms associated with inhalant abuse or attributed to the whims of the patient which is typical of the age category the client falls in.

My advice is to go in for a DAPT in these earlier periods of abuse. Thus precious time could be saved and damages could be detected early.

The points illustrated in the figure given below are diagnostic for Organic Brain Damage. This drawing has been done by a street child abusing Inhalants for more than 3 years now. The said child is 11 years old, a male, studied up to class four before dropping out of school.

The grossly organic indicators were seen consistently present in all Inhalant abusers drawings. The abnormalities in the drawings were proportionately more with greater length of abuse of inhalants.

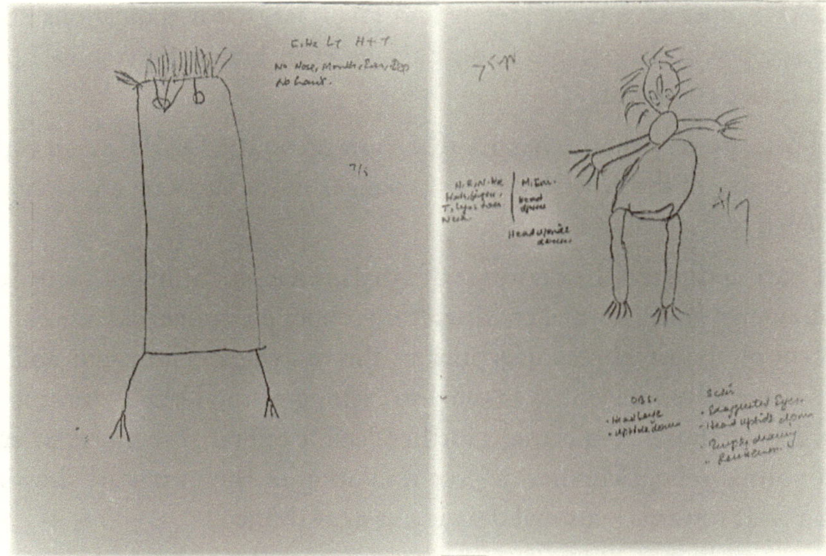

DAPT sketch of an 11 year old Inhalant Abuser   DAPT with HEAD UPSIDE DOWN

Drawing by an Inhalant abuser

with> 5 years of Inhalant abuse

Features of Organic Brain Damage

These have been listed below.

- Large head
- Large figure
- Only head
- Head Upside down.
- Poor proportion
- Omission of parts
- Lines – Simple, heavy
- Lack of details, no details of body
- Erasures frequent.
- Synthesis Weak to Poor.

The percentages of times these signs are likely to be present on DAPT of inhalant abusers (as we found out in our study) are as follows:

Large Head –	60 %
Head Upside down –	7 %
Poor proportions –	60 %
Synthesis poor –	32.5 %
Lack of details –	46.6 %
Omission of parts –	59 %
Only Head –	5 %
Large figure –	32.5 %

The second drawing above shows a figure with head upside down. The patient had a history of inhalant abuse spread for more than five years.

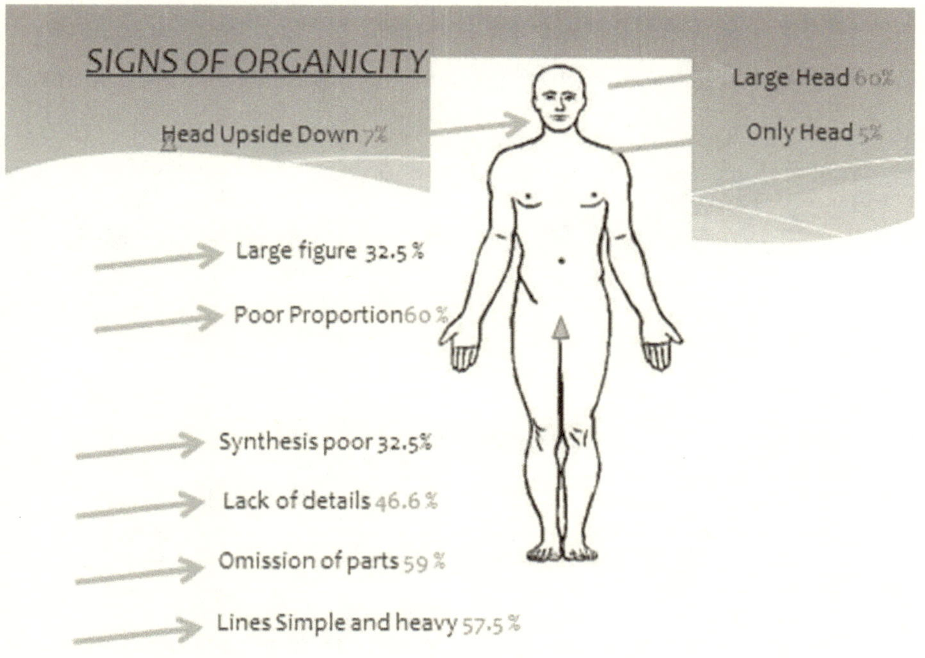

Figure depicting the percentages of presence of the signs for Organic Brain Damage on DAPT

In the table given below we have put up the following categories on x -axis

- *Age distribution of patients*

   5-10 years

   10-15 years,

   15 years and above.

- *Length of inhalant abuse*

   Less than 6 months,

   Between 6 months to 2 years,

   2 to 5 years,

   Above 5 years of drug abuse

On y- axis we have put up the

- Signs on DAPT which are diagnostic of Organic Brain Damage

- The percentage of their presence in the DAPT drawings of our clients.

SIGNS OF ORGANICITY IN INHALANT ABUSERS												
	5-10 YEARS				10-15 YEARS				>15 YEARS			
	<6m	6m-2y	2-5y	>5y	<6m	6m-2y	2-5y	>5y	<6m	6m-2y	2-5y	>5y
Large Head	50%				60%	60%	85%	All			50%	All
Only Head	·		·	·	20%						20%	
Head upside down	50%											50%
Large Figure	50%					50%	42%				20%	
Omission of parts		70%			40%	50%	57%	All			20%	50%
Poor proportion	50%	60%			40%	50%	85%	All			40%	50%
Lines simple heavy		50%			20%	50%	All	All			60%	All
Synthesis poor		30%			40%	20%	42%				40%	50%
Eraser		10%					14%					
Lack of details		30%			20%	40%	71%	All			40%	

The figures in bold show age inappropriate responses due to organic brain damage

We had then compared the drawings of DAPT of inhalant abusers with the DAPT drawings of normal school going children.

SIGNS OF ORGANICITY IN SCHOOL CHILDREN			
	5-7 Years	**7-9 Years**	**9-10 Years**	**10 Years+**
Large Head	66%	50%	42%	40%
-----------	-----------	-----------	-----------	-----------
Only Head	NIL	NIL	NIL	NIL
Head upside down	NIL	NIL	NIL	NIL
-----------	-----------	-----------	-----------	-----------
Large Figure	All	33%		20%
Omission of parts	66%	50%	14.20%	
Poor proportion	All	66%	28.50%	20%
Lines simple heavy	66%	50%	14.20%	60%
Synthesis poor	NIL	NIL	NIL	NIL
Eraser		16.60%	14.50%	
Lack of details	66%	16.60%		

Trends Observed

- *Large Head*– This indicator is consistently present in DAPT of all age group of inhalant users.

  Evidently with increase in duration of inhalant abuse the number of clients drawing a large head increases, suggesting a direct co-relation of inhalants abuse duration and brain degeneration/damage. This is in absence of other factors that could cause brain damage.

  Other factors as nicotine or alcohol abuse are known to cause brain damage but only after many decades of abuse.

  Such rapid development of signs of brain damage is seen in inhalant abusers only.

  History of head injuries and infections of the brain or meninges are also important factors that were ruled out. Exposure to toxic fumes is known to cause brain damage.

  In all the clients that we studied the other contributing factors were ruled out.

Inhalant abusers with six months history of abuse had 60 % (sixty percent) of drawings with large head. With an exposure to inhalants from 7 months to 2 years 85 % (eighty percent) of the drawings had a large head. Finally in patients with a history of more than 3 years of exposure to inhalants all the drawings had the large head. The data was found in inhalant abusers over 10 years of age.

In children between 5 to 10 years age group who had been abusing inhalants the length of usage was not more than 2 years even if they initiated early in life. The comparative drawings for more than 2 years of addiction were not there. However 50 % of the drawings of the patients still showed a large head.

In normal children Large head figures in DAPT shows a gradual resolution as age advances suggesting that there is a normal development of brain.

At 5 years of age 66% of school going children showed a large head which was seen in only 40 % of drawings of children above 10 years

- *Omission of Parts*- Present in all age group of inhalant abusers.

More clients elicit this on DAPT when their duration of exposure is longer in terms of years of abuse. Thus Draw a Person Test of chronic inhalant abusers would definitely have this sign. This is primarily due to-

- Cognitive decline affecting concentration and

- Apathy towards details (characteristic seen in all addictions when intense focus is only on drugs) in the earlier stages.

- Later on it is also partly due to brain damage.

With 6 months of exposure to inhalants 40 %(forty percent) showed omission of parts on the drawings.

With an exposure of 6 months to 2 years it could be seen in 50 %(fifty percent) of the drawings.

Addiction to inhalants from 3 to 5 years had omission of parts in 57 %(fifty seven percent) of the drawings.

Above 5 years of usage all the patients drawing had omission of parts.

In the drawings from school children the drawings showed better comprehension of details as age advanced.

Thus as a normal child grows his drawings show less omission of parts and finally in children above 10 years it becomes rare. As the body image clarifies in a child's mind the drawings become more complete.

Omission of parts was seen in 66 % of 5 year olds and in 14 % of school going children between 9 to 10 years. It was not seen in children at 10 + years of age.

- *Lack of details* – This too shows a strong correlation to length of abuse and is present in DAPT drawings of inhalant abusers early in addiction history. This could be due to subtle cognitive impairment that begins early and is evident clinically when probed meticulously. The decline in cognitive functions in long standing inhalant addiction is a fact that cannot be overemphasized.

This was seen in all the patients in age groups of 10 to 15 years who had abused inhalants for 2 to 5 years and also in the drawings of abusers who had addiction history of more than 5 years.

Lack of details presented in 30 % of Draw a Person Test of 5 to 10 year old who had abused inhalants for more than 6 months.

This was seen in 71 % of 10 to 15 year old who had been abusing inhalants for 6 months to 2 years.

SCHOOL CHILDREN

Amongst the DAPT drawings of normal school going children the following was observed: Between 5 to 7 years of age 66 % of drawings showed lack of details. This came down to 16.6 % in drawings of children aged 8 to 10 years. It was not seen in any drawings of children above 10 years of age.

- *Lines simple and Heavy* – Weak indicator in 5 -10 years age group. In older age groups it is consistently present on Draw a Person Test and increases with increased duration of abuse.

This was seen in all the drawings of inhalant abusers who had a history of abuse for more than 2 years and more than 5 years.

- *Poor proportion* – Seen in drawings of all age groups of inhalant abusers and there seems a definite increase in poor proportions on Draw a Person Test as the chronicity of abuse goes beyond 5 years. With such chronicity the drawings of all the patients lack any normal proportions.

  Below are a detailed percentage wise co-relation of poor proportions in the drawings and the length of inhalant abuse.

  With 6 months addiction 40 % (forty per cent) showed poor proportions

  With 7 months to 2 years 50 % (fifty per cent)

  Between 2 years to five years 85 %(eighty five per cent)

  With abuse history more than 5 years all the drawings had poor proportions.

  When we compare the DAPT drawings of normal school going children on the parameter of poor proportion we see a gradual resolution of the poor proportions as the children grow up. Thus drawings of older school going children show a good sense of proportion. This suggests that brain development is healthy and normal.

Signs of Psychosis on Draw A Person Test

These are enumerated below:

- Omission of important parts.
- Over emphasized eyes, nose, ears, hair or any other part.
- Bizarre additions.
- Scribbling.
- Tiny Empty Drawing.
- Exaggerated size of any part.
- Breasts/breast on the outside of dress
- Sexual organs
- Lack of facial details.
- Profile confusion
- Slanting body

DAPT of a 13 year old inhalant abuser showing: Slanting figure, mammary glands on the outside of the dress, Naval on the outside of the dress, scribbling, profile confusion.

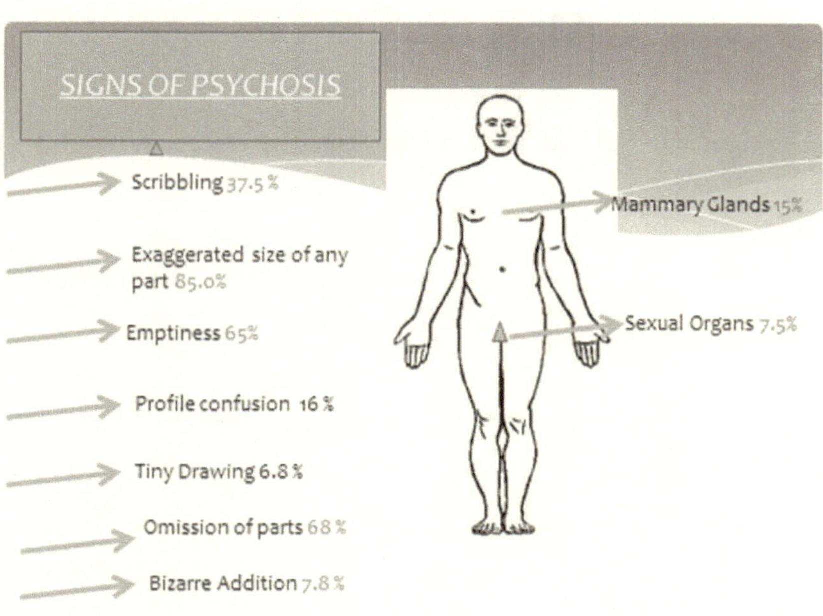

SCRIBBLING - seen in 37.5 % of inhalant abusers

Exaggerated size of any body part - seen in 85.0 % of inhalant abusers

Omission of parts - seen in 68 % of drawings of inhalant abusers

Bizarre additions - seen in 7.8 % of drawings

Profile confusion- seen in 16.5 % of the drawings

Sexual organs - seen in 7.5 % of the drawings of inhalant abusers

Mammary glands - seen in 15 % of the drawings of inhalant abusers

Emptiness - seen in 65 % of the drawings

SIGNS OF PSYCHOSIS IN INHALANT ABUSERS											
AGE	**5-10 YEARS**			**10-15 YEARS**				**>15 YEARS**			
INTAKE PERIOD	<6m	6m-2y	2-5y	<6m	6m-2y	2-5y	>5y	<6m	6m-2y	2-5y	>5y
Omission of parts	16%	**67%**		8.6%	17%	13%	8.6%		11%	26%	**22%**
Bizarre addition		8.3%			4.3%						**11%**
Exaggerated part	16%	**67%**		8.6%	35%	26%	13%		11%	22%	11%
Scribbling	16%	**66%**		4.3%	**8.6%**	**17%**	**17%**			11%	**22%**
Tiny drawing				4.3%			4.3%				**11%**
Sexual organs						4.3%				11%	**22%**
Mammary Glands	16%			8.6%	4.3%		4.3%			11%	**22%**
Empty drawing	**16%**	**67%**		8.6%	13%	13%	8.6%		11%	**22%**	22%
Profile confusion	16%	8.3%				4.3%	4.3%			11%	11%

The figures in bold are age inappropriate responses and point to gross psychotic features

SIGNS OF PSYCHOSIS IN SCHOOL CHILDREN			
	5-7 Years	7-9 Years	9-10 Years	10 Years+
Omission of parts		50%	14%	
Bizarre addition	NIL	NIL	NIL	NIL
Exaggerated part	33%	50%	*57%*	20%
Scribbling			43%	20%
Tiny drawing	33%	16.6%	*28.5%*	20%
Sexual organs	NIL	NIL		NIL
-----------	-----------	-----------	-----------	-----------
Mammary Glands	NIL	NIL		NIL
Empty drawing		50%		
-----------	-----------	-----------	-----------	-----------
Profile confusion			14%	20%

- *Scribbling* as a sign of psychosis shows a co relation with duration of exposure. It has been found consistently on the Draw a Person Test of Inhalants user. Could be one of earliest indicators of Psychosis.

Amongst inhalant abusers in 5 to 10 years of age with 6 months of usage 16 % showed scribbling on their drawings in Draw a Person Test. The scribbling was seen in 60 % of drawings in the abusers who had become chronic and abused inhalants between 6 months to 2 years.

In inhalant abusers between 10 to 15 years of age the ones who were dependent on inhalants for less than 6 months scribbling was seen in 4.3 % of their drawings.

This abnormal sign on Draw a Person Test increased to 8.6 % in subjects who had 6 months to 2 years history of abuse.

In addicts with more than 2 years of history of inhalant abuse the scribbling had increased to 17 % of all drawings.

The Draw Person Test drawings in 15 years and above age group of inhalant abusers showed similar findings. Thus scribbling was found in 11 % of the drawings in abusers who had a dependence history of 2 to 5 years. It had increased to 22 % where the addiction had persisted for more than 5 years.

With abuse of inhalants signs of psychosis as scribbling on the DAPT are showing a direct co-relation to the chronicity of abuse.

- *Conversely the scribbling of normal growing children shows a definite complete resolution over time.*

Comments – In the table above we can see that at 9 to 10 years school going children signs as scribbling or a tiny figure shows an abrupt increase in some. This could be considered as a reflection of pre-pubertal psychological changes that the children undergo. The pre-pubertal age has come down in the past three decades as the exposure to sexual content has increased in movies, media, and advertisements. The social sanctions are more permissive now. Thus having a friend from the opposite sex, dating, free sex, live in relations are all a reality.

- *Exaggerated size of any body part*

This was a single very prominent sign in Draw a Person Test of inhalant abusers. This is more striking in inhalant abusers who are 5 to 10 years old and have been consuming inhalants for at least 6 months to two years duration.

Almost 67 % of the clients translated their body perceptual abnormalities onto their Draw a Person Test. There is a direct co-relation between disturbance in the body image and inhalant use in this formative age group.

These sign *do not* show in any significant numbers in drawings of older age group (10 to 15 years age). Even after chronic use the body image seems to be maintained.

- *Sexual Organs* – as seen on Draw a Person Test of chronic users.

A very interesting trend is observed. The moment an inhalant abuser enters his teens i.e. between 10 to 15 years of age his drawings show sexual organs in 11 % of cases. However with growing teens as the inhalant abuser crosses 15 years of age nearly 22 % of the drawings show sexual organs.

The sexual drive has commenced and is very powerful. This explains the addicts pre-occupation with sex organs. However no control on drives points towards a psychotic trend. The drawing of sexual organs on the outside depicts a loss of social inhibition.

The school going teenagers DAPT drawings do not show sex organs despite a strong drive in this teenage group as well.

Mammary Glands depiction seen in chronic users especially in the age group of 15 years and above. With inhalant abuse of up to 2 years the depiction of mammary glands was seen in 11 % of Draw a Person Test drawings. With the abuse history of more than 2 years .i.e. 2 to 5 years the % of drawings showing mammary glands was 22 %.

- Depiction of *Nipples* in the drawings is seen more often with longer usage of inhalants.

  These are not seen in Draw a Person Test drawings of normal children

- *Empty Drawings* seen more frequently in inhalant abusers

  In 5 – 10 years age group and above 15 years age group who have been abusing inhalants.

  In Normal children seen only in 7–10 years age group.

Signs on Draw A Person Test for Neurosis

- Thin/Heavy Lines
- Broken lines.
- Placement of figure on the paper.
- Shading of any part
- Over exaggerated Eyes, Teeth.
- Posture of the figure.
- Tiny Figure
- Tiny Hands/Large hands
- Short Arms/Long Arms
- Omissions of parts
- Poor Integration.

DAPT of a 16 year old girl showing signs as: Shading of a body part, tiny hands, over emphasis on hair and neck, missing eyebrows.

EMOTIONAL INDICATORS IN INHALANT ABUSERS		
	5-10 Years	10-15 Years	>15 Years
INTEGRATION	54%	25%	**37.00%**
ASYMMETRY	27%	40%	**50.00%**
SLANTING FIGURE		5%	
TRANSPARENCY	18%	15%	**25%**
TINY FIGURE	18%	15%	**37%**
HANDS CUT OFF	27%	10%	12.50%
NO BODY	54%	35%	**12.5%**
-----------	-----------	-----------	-----------
NO NECK	72%	**60%**	**100%**

The figures in bold show indicate an inappropriate response suggesting neurosis

EMOTIONAL INDICATORS IN SCHOOL CHILDREN			
	5-7 Years	7-10 Years	>10 Years
INTEGRATION			
ASYMMETRY	100%	54%	NIL
SLANTING FIGURE			
TRANSPARENCY			
TINY FIGURE		9%	14%
HANDS CUT OFF	20%		
NO BODY			
-----------	-----------	-----------	-----------
NO NECK	20%	36%	

8 Emotional indicators were significantly more often on the Draw a Person Test of INHALANT abusers at various age levels than in the normal.

Poor Integration- Weak Synthesis in the drawings was seen in 38% of Inhalant abusers as compared to NIL in normal age. Quite similar results are found (poor integrative capacity, immaturity, impulsivity, poor co-ordination) in drawings of Brain injured individuals. Forty four percent (44%) of (Brain Injury) patients showed poor integration versus only 5 % of normal in a study by Koppitz.

Gross asymmetry of limbs- Significant in all age groups of Inhalant Abusers and an increasing trend with longer duration of exposure.

With 6 months to 2 years of exposure to inhalants 27 % of 10 ten year olds,

39 % of 10 to 15 year olds and

50 % of 15 years and above showed asymmetry in limbs in their drawings. This also correlates to findings in a study by Teznikoff and Tomblen 1956 ("shrunken limbs") where draw a person test of brain injured individuals was analysed.

This was not seen in the drawings of the normal individuals.

Slanting of figure of more than 15 degrees was seen in 5 % of drawings of inhalant abusers vs. nil % of drawings of normal.

Seen in insecure and unstable children.

Interestingly about 15 % Brain Injury patient show slanting of figure vs. 2 % Normal as per a study by Kopitz.

Transparencies. This is found in drawings of 20 % of Inhalant Abusers as against NIL in normal individuals drawings. It is more primitive associated with immaturity and concrete thinking. Co incidentally in a study similar results were found when drawings of brain damaged were compared to those of normal. Significantly 11 % Brain Injured showed this abnormality as against only 1% of normal.

This definitely points to the fact that there has been some degree of neurological damage with inhalant abuse over a period of time. Transparencies in the drawings are a sign which may have importance in pointing to this brain damage.

Tiny figure Less than 2 inches found in 12% of drawings of inhalant abusers versus only 3% in normal individual at same age .More an indication of timidity and depression. Reflects a lack of self-confidence and self-esteem.

Cut-off hands – Inhalant abuser drawings show cut off hands in 17% of drawings as compared to just 5% in the drawings of the normal. Interpretation similar as in tiny figure interpretation. Also depicts general attitude of concern and guilt.

Omission of body parts –Normal till 6 years of age. My findings are that the omission of body is present on Draw a Person Test of abusers at all ages thus it shows a *pathology in progress* in the brain. Study by (Gordon) on Brain Injury clients suggests slow brain development.

Omission of neck – Found in 29 %(twenty nine percent) of the drawings of inhalant abusers. This is seen in only 7 %(seven percent) of the drawings of normal individuals. Especially at ages 10 -12 yrs. Depicts impulsivity and lack of control a significant finding in neurological cases.

COMMENTS - The features on Neurosis as depicted in the drawings of inhalant abusers results from direct action of the chemical in the inhalant (toluene, benzene etc.) on the brain tissue. The chemical is toxic and causes neuronal death on sustained exposure. The second reason for neuronal assault and damage is due to Anoxia induced by the inhalant rush every time it is inhaled (huffing, puffing).

Controversies of Draw A Person Test

The controversies that shroud interpretation of DAPT are its first limitations. The issues of *validity* and *reliability* have been the questioned. Then the *contextual influences* as the race and sex of the tester could influence the interpretations. Another argument against DAPT is that it claims to test many mental aspects and abnormalities and therefore stands to questions.

The test however has stood on due to its *unique* quality of easiness to administer. The results can stand up to reliability and validity when used correctly. It does give good indication for many mental aspects. However we have to follow the *empathic model* while interpreting Draw a Person Test to be more connected with our subject's mental state.

It is a *standardised test* which adds to its credibility.

TREATMENT OF INHALANT ABUSE

TREATMENT AND MEDICAL CARE

The medical care of patients with inhalant-related psychiatric disorders encompasses services of many areas of medical specialists.

Also the team of medical professionals must work in unison with clinical psychologist, social workers neurologist, and peer counselors to ensure that every aspect of the treatment plan is fulfilled.

Patients require hospitalization for better results.

First due to the fact that a person undergoing detoxification in an outpatient care is very easily tempted to take inhalant in one form or the other at home. The patient is used to having his ways at home. The attendants are also used to accepting his demands. Thus the addict procures his stuff or forces his attendant to get it for him. The addiction makes a person very cunning and if he has consumed the inhalant during treatment then the effort has been undone. The treatment has now failed.

Once an addict consumes the inhalant he experiences the much wanted high. Under the influence of the high his insight to his illness is lost and craving takes over. His mind now becomes deceiving and he manipulates and cheats the caretaker and the treating team. He makes up stories, lies and continues with his drug taking behavior.

Hospitalization is all the more important as the patient could have severe with drawl symptoms. The delirious, suicidal, homicidal, or gravely disabled patients require hospital care. As inpatients, they may require the administration of medications to relieve any abnormal behavior due to psychosis resulting from the chemicals inhaled.

Proper medications, food and consistent medical care are possible only in an inpatient set up.

Counseling (supportive therapy) should be initiated, along with patient education to explain the dangers of consuming inhalants. Evaluate patients for psychiatric comorbidity.

No controlled studies have been performed to guide the treatment of patients who abuse inhalants and who have inhalant dependence. Additionally, no specific medications have been researched by the pharmaceutical industry which is available for detoxification of inhalant dependence.

Programs and specialized centers that specifically treat inhalant abuse are rare and difficult to find. Therefore, treatment planning most often is tailored much like that of the treatment of patients with chemical dependence.

The Steps of Treatment of Inhalant Abuse

1. History taking in every detail. We have highlighted it in previous chapters.

2. Clinical examination- a detailed and thorough clinical assessment as detailed earlier goes a long way in giving good outcome to the treatment. The evaluation also helps to ascertain the presence of any co-morbid psychiatric illness.

3. Neurological assessment

   INVESTIGATIONS

4. Laboratory testing as enlisted in previous chapters

5. Neuropsychological testing

1. Abstinence

This is the most important pre-condition to successful treatment. The patient needs to be sincere and committed to stay away from inhalants and focus only on treatment for his betterment. In cases where the patient cannot keep his urge under check, supervision by family member or the hospital staff (if getting treatment at a hospital) round the clock is of paramount importance.

The hospital staff makes it a point to check the visitors' person and belongings so that they may not smuggle in any inhalant. This usually happens when the family member is over indulgent and blind to the seriousness of the outcome of their own action. They want to give patient some relief or are doing such acts under threat from the patient.

It is known where families members are allowed to stay with the patient in the detoxification centers as their attendant the chances of drugs being smuggled into the center are very high. Even if one keeps paid attendants the chances exist as the addict is an old hand at manipulating people for his needs. Thus centers where family members are not allowed are able to overcome this pilferage.

2. Detoxification

Detoxification is the process of allowing the body to rid itself of a drug while managing the symptoms of withdrawal. It is the first step in a drug treatment program.

This is done in a hospital set up in severe addictions where profound withdrawals are expected which cannot be cared for at home.

The detoxification should also be followed by treatment with a behavioral-based therapy and/or medication. Detoxification alone with no follow-up does not qualify as treatment.

In-patient detoxification has the following benefits:

- Patient is in a protected setting where he/she are away from drugs.

- Detoxification process becomes safer under the expert medical team and its supervision.

- Completion of detoxification process is rapid as adequate medications can be given under direct medical supervision.

- Multi-specialty services are available twenty four hours daily to attend to concurrent medical conditions and complications, if they arise.

Out-patient detoxifications has benefits in selected cases which are – high on motivation, have good social and family support. These are medically manageable (at home) for mild withdrawals of inhalant abuse .The advantages of out-patient detoxification are:

- They are cheap

- They do not disturb the patient's routine

- The patient does not undergo an abrupt change from a protected atmosphere of the hospital setting into the outside world after the treatment. The patient is undertaking treatment at home, stays at home attends to daily chores and thus there is no change in atmosphere during treatment and post treatment.

Patients who are addicted to inhalants experience withdrawal symptoms similar to those of any other patient addicted to drugs. These symptoms are unbearable and troublesome to the patient. The withdrawal symptoms in inhalant dependence are usually tremors, chills, sweats, cramps, confusion, nausea, and hallucinations. In some cases seizures can be expected.

Detoxification from inhalants typically lasts longer than detox from alcohol and other drugs due to the fact that inhalants are stored in body's fatty tissues and take a lot of time to get eliminated from the body.

Detoxification Protocol

There is no protocol and the treatment has to be individualized. Besides taking care of withdrawal symptoms and the co-morbid conditions the detoxification must at all times take care of-

Nutrition: Most of the inhalant abusers suffer from nutritional deficiencies which must be corrected with proper regular diet.

Hydration and Electrolytes: inhalant abuse results in electrolyte imbalances and dehydration. Intravenous fluids as normal saline, dextrose normal saline, Ringer lactate or any other appropriate infusion has to be given to correct the water and electrolyte imbalances. Serum electrolytes should be monitored till such time that they are stabilized. After wards a serum electrolyte check is required at the time of discharge. They may be done if hydration of the patient is not proper due to weather conditions or body fluid loss in loose motions and vomiting.

Hygiene: often the hygiene being very poor the addicts are infested with ticks, scabies or have psoriasis, dermatitis and rashes on the body. Proper treatment is aimed at taking care of these conditions. The patient may even be isolated so as not to infect other inmates.

In such cases a cross reference to a dermatologist is done and these skin conditions and infestations/infections are taken care of under his expertise.

Medications for Detoxification

For an uncomplicated case of inhalant abuse these are used to take care of withdrawal symptoms–

- Anti-emetics for taking care of nausea and vomiting.

- Busiprone to take care of anxiety.

- Propranolol to counter tremors and agitation.

- Divalproex, Oxcarbazepine for seizures.

Once the patient is detoxified, evaluate for other psychiatric illnesses.

No medications should be used unless a treatable diagnosis has been identified.

- If the patient has depression independent of the inhalant abuse, treat with the antidepressant of choice.

- If the patient abuses alcohol in addition to inhalants, disulfiram (Antabuse) or naltrexone can be used in appropriate settings (with normal Liver Function Test)

- If the patient is diagnosed with co-morbid attention-deficit/ hyperactivity disorder, a psychostimulant such as Atomoxetine, Methylphenidate, can be used for treatment.

- If the patient is psychotic as a result of the inhalant abuse *(inhalant-induced psychosis)*, the psychiatrist may use an appropriate antipsychotic such as haloperidol (Haldol) or risperidone (Risperdal), with or without a benzodiazepine. This is at the discretion of the psychiatrist who has to assess the merits and indications of any particular antipsychotic or tranquilizers.

- If the patient has an *inhalant-induced mood disorder,* detoxification is recommended without using anti-depressants. The use of anti-depressants is indicated only if the depression persists for longer than 2-4 weeks after withdrawal. Usually Serotonin Specific Reuptake Inhibitors (SSRI) as Escitalopram is helpful. Other medicines could be Paroxetine, Fluoxetine. Second in line would be TCAs (Tricyclic Antidepressants). Mood stabilizers may also be prescribed to take care of any mood switch that may occur with anti-depressants.

- Detoxification for patients who are experiencing *inhalant-induced anxiety*:

  The use of sedatives or antianxiety medications is contraindicated (experience of western countries) because inhalant intoxication can worsen if the patient relapses and starts abusing inhalants when he is still on anti-anxiety medication.

  In our experience we find use of anti-anxiety agents to be very useful to reduce anxiety whether primary or secondary to inhalant abuse. In just the minimal dose required it can be used judiciously and withdrawn safely. It needs to be stopped if patient has relapsed. In fact other medications as antidepressants, antabuse, and others too are to be withdrawn if the patient starts reusing inhalants.

Next, a peer system is established.

Under the supervision of a psychiatrist/psychologist the patient attends group therapy sessions. The patient's sense of acceptance and belonging to a group is established. A patient knows he is not alone in the problem of inhalant abuse. The groups support and interactions are beneficial when the meetings are done regularly in an in-patient set-up.

The patient should also regularly take active part in group therapy sessions. He has to be put on rational emotive therapy, and cognitive behavior therapy.

Once the patient has undergone in-patient program he benefits from self-help groups in the outside world. These are carried out at fixed places on fixed days in most major and small cities. The patients must on regular basis attend these peer support, generated in 12-step programs/Smart recovery groups/chemical dependency self-help groups.

Once these two tasks are accomplished namely the detoxification and the peer group set-up, assess the patient for physical, cognitive, and neurologic problems. If any problems are noted in these areas, they must be treated immediately by a specialist. Regular evaluation by these specialists at constant intervals is required to monitor improvement and suggest any further interventions if needed.

Identify any psychological strength the patient has and build on these strengths to create confidence and self-respect in the patient.

The group therapy focuses on faulty attitudes the patient developed during his growing years in his social milieu which contribute to his addictive behavior. Contributing to the addictive behavior is a list of Character Defects. These defects are part and parcel of a personality type the "Addict Personality". These personality traits generate anxiety, frustration and maladjustments.

The prominent defects of character are discussed thread bare in the group daily to bring insight in the inhalant abuser. The other addicts in the group also share their character defects and how they are trying to overcome it. Some major character defects are enumerated below-

<u>Anxiety</u> – Not as a clinical diagnosis, this is a faulty way of viewing things with an eye toward what is wrong, what might be wrong, what has been wrong or what is going to be wrong. Excessive worry, especially about things I cannot change.

<u>Arrogance</u> – an egoistic stand in every situation proves a big hindrance in understanding any situation. It hampers concern for others and spoils relations.

<u>Controlling behavior</u> – expecting others to follow the patient's whims and fancies. Being demanding and childlike sometimes in an obstinate manner, behaving illogically.

<u>Dishonesty</u> – Telling lies, hiding things, telling half-truths or pretending something is so that isn't. Withholding important information. Adding untrue details to stories and situations. Stealing, cheating, taking things that aren't ours and that we aren't entitled to.

<u>Dependence</u> emotionally on others

<u>Fear</u>

<u>Gluttony, greed,</u> – Wanting and taking too much: food, sex, time, money, comfort, leisure, material possessions, attention, and security. Acquiring things at the expense of others.

<u>Gossiping</u> – Speaking or writing about others in a negative manner, especially to get them in trouble or to feel superior to them and bond with someone else against the target of the gossip.

<u>Intolerance of others</u> – Not accepting people as they are.

<u>Impatience</u> – Being frustrated by waiting, wanting often to be some time in the future, wanting something to change or improve rather than accepting it as it is.

<u>Inventory taking and being judgmental</u> – Noticing and listing, out loud or to themselves, the faults of others.

<u>Jealousy.</u>

<u>Laziness, procrastination</u> – Putting things off repeatedly. Not carrying our own load as much as we are able. Letting others provide things for us that we ought to get for ourselves

<u>Prejudice, perfectionism</u>

<u>Resentment, rigidity</u>

<u>Rationalizations</u> justifying wrong deeds by saying one had good intentions. Not accepting blame.

<u>Self-centeredness,</u> self-pity – spending considerable time, thinking about myself, with no regard for others

The patient becomes aware of his defects in group meetings and is given tasks which can help overcome them. Overcoming the character defects is a daily voluntary effort on the part of the patient. It has to be carried out with all awareness throughout life.

Address any other problems they may have. The goals are to return the patient to the community with a drug-free peer network and to continue or enhance self-support.

Discuss safe sex with the patient, including partner precautions and birth control. Financial issues are also discussed with the client and his family members where necessary.

In addition, the family should receive education about the disorder, secure substances that could be huffed, and become familiar with local mental health laws regarding commitment policies.

Any other family member who is drug dependent or alcohol dependent requires concurrent treatment as detoxification and counseling.

The family members should attend regularly the family therapy sessions.

A thorough assessment of family structure, stability, and dynamics must be a major component of any treatment program addressing the inhalant abuser. Family involvement is critically important. Treatment is focused on the therapeutic interventions necessary with the family. These help in providing education about inhalants, better bonding, improved social skill, and good communication with the patient.

With disjointed, disturbed families regular counseling is required. The highly estranged family atmosphere is a deterrent for recovery of an inhalant addict. The communication abnormalities that exist in such families are taken up with each member individually and in family counseling with all the members. The trouble brewing behaviors of the members, the impractical expectations from each other, and the impatience for each other are all addressed.

Often it has been necessary to isolate a particular member whose presence cannot be handled by the newly recovered patient.

Family counseling helps the parents, caretakers/guardians to understand their own behavior patterns which directly encourages or precipitates addictive behavior and finally addiction in vulnerable recovering addicts. It also helps them overcome their own anxieties in general and specific in relation to the patient.

They are given insight through counseling to overcome their undue tendencies of showering love on the recovering addict. Their overindulgence with the patient's whims, over demanding behavior and then giving in to patient's manipulative behavior are major concerns of counseling. They are also counseled to overcome their depression which they experience out of guilt when they do not comply with the patients demands.

They have been harboring a defective behavior towards their patient. There is a persistent and parasitic nature to this relationship. The caretaker usually the parents, sibling, wife or even a friend satisfies his own deep-seated needs for love and attention by being pre-occupied and overtly indulgent with the addict, his addiction, and self-centered behavior. The care taker foregoes his own priorities by painfully pushing himself/herself to help the addict.

It becomes their mission to do something to make a significant change in the patient's life. These people are called CO-DEPENDENTS and their dependence is on the patient. It would be correct to say *they are addicted to the patient who is addicted to chemicals*.

Codependency is a type of dysfunctional helping relationship where one person supports or enables another person's drug addiction and other behavior arising therefrom. Co-dependency is also seen in case of attendants who look after individuals suffering from alcoholism, gambling addiction, poor mental health, immaturity, irresponsibility, or under-achievement.

Among the core characteristics of codependency, the most common theme is an excessive reliance on other people for approval and a sense of identity. The codependency behavior has very deep subconscious moorings. Co-dependency can be characterized as a *subclinical and situational or episodic behavior similar to that of dependent personality disorder*.

Some users of the codependency concept use the word as an alternative to using the concept of *dysfunctional families*.

In its broadest definition, a codependent is someone who cannot function from their innate self and whose thinking and behavior is instead organized around another person, and his addiction. It requires one person to be physically and/or psychologically addicted to a chemical such as cannabis, alcohol, heroin, inhalants, and a second person to be psychologically dependent to the first person's behavior with a motive to get his love, to make a difference in his life, or to be appreciated by him.

We can identify such persons in our own lives and families.

The Ten Characteristics of Co-Dependent Behavior Briefed Below

Feeling responsible for solving others' problems:

The codependent feels the need to solve another's problems. The codependent believes that help is needed and that the person in need cannot manage to make the right decisions or take the right actions to solve his or her own problems. Without the codependent's input, disaster for the other suffering person is assured.

Offering advice to others whether it is asked for or not:

The codependent jumps at the opportunity to provide much-needed advice. The codependent offers an endless stream of good advice regardless of whether the advice has been asked for or not.

Expecting others to do what the co-dependent says:

Once advice has been given, the codependent expects the advice to be followed. Codependents often do not understand boundaries and easily enter ego boundaries of significant ones to the point of being overbearing and irritable.

Feeling used and unappreciated for all the codependent does:

The codependent will expend enormous amounts of energy to take charge of another's life-all under the guise of sincerely wanting to help. When the help or advice is ignored or rejected, the codependent feels angry, abused, and unappreciated.

Trying to please people so others will like or love the codependent:

Codependents will go out of their way to please another, hoping to receive love, approval, or be accepted and liked. If the approval is not given, the codependent will feel victimized.

Taking everything personally:

Because there are little or no boundaries in the codependent's life. Any remark, comment or action is a reflection back upon the codependent. Such comments are taken in utmost seriousness as personal demotions. This leads to more indulgence on the part of the co-dependent who would now make more efforts to do things which would not bring criticism to him/her. This makes the need to feel in control paramount.

Feeling like a victim:

Everything that happens either to the codependent or the loved one is a reflection on the codependent. For everything that happens to anybody in the family the co-dependent feels responsible. Such people usually feel victimized and powerless when things don't work their way. They do not understand their role in creating their own reality.

Using manipulation, shame, or guilt to control others' behavior:

To get their way codependents will respond in a fashion that will force compliance by others. These tactics may be subconscious. Since everyone else's behavior is a reflection on the codependent and his prestige it is important that the codependent feel in control and thus feel un-criticized, faultless, and important.

Lying to themselves and making excuses for others' bad behavior

Because codependents do not deal directly with their own feelings, they develop techniques to lie to themselves about others' behaviors. Because they feel responsible for addict's behaviors, they will rationalize and blame some other people for their loved one's (addicts) poor behavior. They may blame themselves for another's poor behavior thus inciting guilt in others and seeking to maintain control.

Fearing rejection and being unlovable

The codependent fears that if he or she is not successful at everything, or indeed expresses his/her feelings or needs, they will be rejected. In a codependent's way of thinking, he or she will be unlovable. A codependent does not trust others easily or share openly with others because he or she is fearful of getting exposed.

Even if the addict has recovered the co-dependents concern does not seem to wane off and the uncalled for, sick indulgence with the addict continues. This is a big hindrance in recovery and eventually could lead to relapse.

The co-dependent is given counseling quite similar to the counseling given to addicts so that they can overcome their own weaknesses and defective behavior patterns.

Factors Responsible for Sustenance of Addiction to Inhalants

The role of various factors which are responsible for maintaining addiction in an individual is very vital for the psychiatrists and mental health team to know and to deal with during the course of treatment. These factors relate to the patients environment, and patients own vulnerabilities to relapse. A good environment and a personality with positive defenses are also responsible for recovery of an addict.

The patient's own attitudes, personality defects have been the greatest stumbling block in addiction treatment. However when the patient is in the therapeutic milieu for a long time he/she is put on regular group and individual counseling besides other tasks that help the patient understand their defects better in addition to learning coping skills for future.

The external factors are

- Persistent stress at home
- Persistent stress at work

- Presence of any member in family who is abusing drugs
- Peers and friends who are abusing drugs.

The above mentioned factors relate to a patients social, mental, emotional and economic life. All are very important and all take some time to be sorted out. Sometimes they just would not get all right. The psychiatrist, counselors and the peer counselor work all along and make efforts through discussions to at least gear up the individuals coping skills which would help him overcome all other adversities even if they persist.

If the patient cannot maintain sobriety, the psychiatrist should consider residential treatment options, which can last anywhere from 3-12 months. In many clients with high risk of relapse, rehabilitation treatment is strongly advised.

REHABILITATION OF INHALANT ABUSERS

Rehabilitation centers offer treatment for drug addiction through long term admission usually 3 months to 12 months. These centers work on programs specially designed to treat the maladaptive patterns of behavior associated with drug addiction either as their cause or their effects.

The program originally meant for drug addicts and alcoholics has to be individualized and tailor made for the inhalant abuser. The inhalant abusers are more difficult to handle as they have poor attention span, are disruptive and resistant to treatment.

The inhalant abuser is a recluse but has great binding with another inhalant abuser. This is taken advantage of and "peer patient advocate" system is put in the treating format where the "peer patient advocate" teaches the newcomer the "ropes to recovery".

THERAPEUTIC   COMMUNITY   PROGRAM   FOR REHABILITATION

According to Therapeutic Community (TC) program the substance use disorder erodes social, vocational skills and family ties and positive skills for good life. The TC program helps the person re-learn and re-establish the positive skills and also gain a physically and mentally healthy life. For some it is the first exposure to an orderly life and habilitation that is learning for the first time behavioral skills, values, attitudes associated with healthy and functional living.

TC is a highly regulated daily program with clear expectations from the inmates the behavior expected and rewards for effort at working hard to achieve the goal. Disciplinary sanctions help to maintain structure for staff and participants. Thus the small society of the therapeutic community is orderly and productive.

Routines include morning and evening meetings, group meetings, recreation, work assignment, personal leisure time. Work is an essential part of therapeutic community program.

Each participant is assigned a task to teach him/her sense of responsibility, the importance of self-reliance, respect for work and value of accountability. It helps take personal responsibility and accountability for every action that a patient takes in future. Vocational and educational activities in the group provide work, communications and interpersonal skill training.

The inmates who have fared very well on their assignments are given a higher rank and some privileges along with greater responsibilities. Thus those who have been promoted are viewed as role models. They are examples of "Right Living". They have to "pull up" other inmates who have not yet learnt positive social living. Living in a therapeutic community also brings about a mutual self-help attitude. Each action of mutual help is seen as a chance of developing skills. The individual becomes compassionate to emotions of others (a trait absent in addicts). Care and concern for others thus starts growing in the individual. It helps develop positive social interactions, and bonding which helps develop social network.

Community meetings (morning prayers, group discussions) help review goals, procedures and community functioning. TC participants are encouraged to take accountability and set goals for their own well-being and positive participation in the community when they leave the center.

An important therapeutic goal of the TC program is to help inmates identify their feelings, emotions and learn to express them in positive and acceptable ways in society.

The participants in the Therapeutic community program pass through three stages at the completion of their treatment.

In the first stage the participant absorbs himself totally in the program, taking responsibility and attending to daily routines. Living in a drug free milieu also helps him break ties with his previous life attitudes and drug taking behavior and helps replace them with more socially fruitful and accepted behavior.

In the second stage evidence based treatment modalities as CBT (Cognitive Behavior Therapy), and Motivational interviewing are done to enhance the benefits of the "community method".

The overall goal is to bring about a change in attitude and behavior to instill hope, emotional growth, and strengthen self-management ability. The other areas that require attention and resolving are issues in a person's personal life, vocational life, and one's psychological and familial needs.

In the third stage the patient prepares for his separation from the therapeutic community and entry into the outside larger community seeking employment education or vocation with the TC help.

However the therapeutic community provides an after care support system as recovery is an ongoing process. This is done by arranging individual counseling, family counseling in the follow-up period after discharge. They are also required to attend self-help meetings (Alcoholic anonymous or Narcotic anonymous).

Rehabilitation Centers Based on 12-Step Recovery Program of Alcoholics Anonymous

Twelve steps of Alcoholics Anonymous is a fellowship of suffering alcoholics who have been guided through its principles and have been able to lead an alcohol free sober life. It has been a Gospel of sorts, a Guide which has helped millions of suffering alcoholics all over the world to overcome their problem for last eight decades.

Alcoholics Anonymous (AA), the first twelve-step fellowship, was founded in 1935 by Bill Wilson and Dr. Robert Holbrook Smith, known to AA members as "Bill W." and "Dr. Bob", in Akron, Ohio. In 1946 they formally established the twelve traditions to help deal with the issues of how various groups could relate to common problems faced by them in alcoholism and function as members supporting each other. The practice of remaining anonymous (using only ones first names) when interacting with the general public was published in the first edition of the AA Big Book.

The set of guiding principles which outline a course of action for tackling alcohol problems have also been useful for drug addiction and compulsions. However with inhalant abusers the program has to be tailor made and individualized keeping in view the very specific needs of the individual.

The 12 steps of this program are given in Appendix 2

Rehab centers which incorporate 12 step recovery programs admit patients for variable periods of 3 to 6 months or even longer.

It is a drug free zone and has a well-defined daily schedule for the participants. The patients are taken in after their detoxification which has been done in a hospital set-up.

The daily routine includes morning prayers, yoga or simple exercises, breakfast, then morning meetings usually for reading out current affairs. Then there are group meetings to discuss responsibilities to be given to individuals. The participants have to write down their individual moral inventories daily and share when asked to with their sponsors. A sponsor is much like the senior in a TC program whose responsibility is to help out the sponsee with his individual problems.

A person's behavior and taking or neglecting responsibilities for the group are openly discussed in the meetings along with ideas and suggestions to improve upon such behaviors.

The core issues discussed repeatedly are -

POWELESSNESS on alcohol/drugs: The addict begins to understand she or he is powerless over the drugs or alcohol. The struggle not to drink begins to slip away. Gradually, attention starts to shift from the substance to focus on oneself and ones defects.

The first stage of coming out of denial is to acknowledge that there is a problem; second, that it is a life-threatening problem over which one is powerless; and third, that actually the problem lies in one's own attitudes and behavior.

WILLINGNESS to accept defects and take steps to bring about a change.

Willingness involves putting down all guards at self-defense and self- justifications of ones grossly abnormal behavior before and during addiction. Now there is an increasing awareness and observation of one's dysfunctional behavior and addiction(s) – what is referred to as "insanity" in the AA language. This crucial development signifies the genesis of an observing ego. Now one begins to exercise some restraint over addictive and undesirable habits, words, and deeds. The Program works behaviorally as well as spiritually.

Abstinence and forbearance from old behavior are accompanied by anxiety, anger and a sense of loss of control. New, preferable attitudes and behavior (often called "contrary action") feel uncomfortable, and arouse other emotions, including fear and guilt. One's "complexes" are being challenged and taken care of. As newer order of routine, responsibility, relationship and attitude is accepted the old patterns of misfit behaviors wear off.

Group support is important in reinforcing new behavior, because the emotions triggered by these changes are very powerful and can retard and even arrest recovery. Additionally, resistance to the changed behavior is experienced from family, and friends for the very same reasons. The anxiety and resistance may be so great that the addict or abuser may go back to drinking or using.

UNMANAGEABLE life and everything connected with life as maintaining routine, job, food, family, and finances becomes unmanageable. Regular sessions are taken on unmanageability with every inmate penning down instances of *Unmanageability* in his life. There is a huge sharing of personal experiences in the group. This helps the inmate to accept the losses that the drug taking behavior caused.

Discussion also focuses on how to restore what has been lost. Some things are lost permanently and it is accepted as one's own folly. The group supports the individual on such traumatic issues by sharing their own self-made history of tragedies, setbacks and the ways they coped with it.

***CHARACTER** defects:* sessions on defects of character focuses on what one is doing habitually. These are acts of commission or omissions that are unsocial, self-centered and disruptive to put it briefly and have grown with the patient to become an inseparable part of him.

These defects are a manifestation of wrong attitudes in the environs that is bringing up the child. In such environs the child develops self-centeredness, leading to demanding behavior, which overlooks the respect, emotions and needs of others. It becomes disruptive for the family members. This is the "King Baby Syndrome" where a person wants what he wants and he wants it right away at any cost. This low frustration tolerance and the resentment that it brings is doused by any drug that offers sedation and an escape from the emotional turmoil.

The character defect thus forms a soil for all types of addictive, often anti-social behavior.

The therapy inculcates "contrary action" for every such action as mentioned above on repeated basis till a more socially positive behavior and attitude takes over.

RESENTMENTS- The patient has deep seated resentment for people who he believes have wronged him at some juncture in life. Some of these are genuine and many of them are not correct because the patient has interpreted the actions of his loved ones with a self-centered, selfish, and egoistic temperament. The inmate is asked to enlist them and openly discuss them out with the sponsor.

A meaningful objective dialogue helps to correct many wrong perceptions and perspectives which have ailed the individual thus far. The individual has strained relationship which is usually brittle and distraught. The individual's impatience, expectations from others, demanding attitude, controlling behavior, disrespect, suspiciousness, jealousy are all in the undercurrent of their relationship.

A sustained effort by the counselors and the team brings about the change. With newly acquired attitudes, behavior and philosophy the patient often faces strange responses from people who have known him in the past. Often these reactions of other people to the changes in the patient are very disappointing and lead to frustration in the patient who requires support and counseling at any time of the day should such a need arise.

The patient has to seek help at the earliest and not harbor resentment.

Even though the 12 step program does not recommend punishment but many centers have to improvise such punishments as taking away privileges for irresponsible behavior in any form as dereliction of duty, breaking the house decorum, engaging in inappropriate behavior.

Conversely good appropriate behavior is rewarded with privileges

The patients who are to be discharged may require a half-way home for some time to acclimatize to the outside world before finally making it outside.

On regular follow-ups, physical assessments, investigations are done when required. Usually follow-ups focus on stressful issues in the patient's life and his coping skills. They also take the family counseling in the ambit.

Peer support in the outside world is gained by attending fellowship meetings as *Narcotic Anonymous, Chemical Dependency self-help groups, Smart Recovery groups* regularly and helps sustain recovery.

WORLD WIDE GRIM PICTURE AND THE LAW

More than 22 million Americans age 12 and older have used inhalants and every year more than 750,000 use inhalants for the first time. The poison control centers across US have record number of children aged 12 and under (70000 from 2011 to 2014) who had ingested, inhaled or rubbed hand sanitizers to get a "high". Despite the substantial prevalence and serious toxicities of inhalant use, it has been termed *the forgotten epidemic.* Inhalant abuse remains the least-studied form of substance abuse, although research on its epidemiology, neurobiology, treatment, and prevention has accelerated in recent years.

According to the European School Project on Alcohol and Other Drugs, 20% of youth in the 12 to 16 age group have tried inhalants.

In Nairobi, Kenya, an estimated 60,000 children live on the streets and almost all are addicted to some sort of inhalant.

In the Pakistani city of Karachi there are an estimated 14,000 street kids, of whom 80% to 90% sniff glue or solvents.

About 5 percent of all deaths in teenagers in England and Wales are now caused by VSA (volatile substance abuse). The phenomenon, what was then called 'Etheromania', although essentially an urban and middle class one was considered sufficiently serious to trigger governmental reaction.

Although inhalants are not regulated under the Controlled Substances Act, thirty-eight states in the US have placed restrictions on the sale and distribution to minors of certain products that are commonly abused as inhalants. Some states have introduced fines, incarceration for sale and possession of specified inhalants and also mandatory treatment for use of inhalant chemicals.

Laws also exist in some US states prohibiting the recreational inhalation of nitrous oxide.

Some communities in Western Australia and South Australia have passed local laws making petrol sniffing an offense. In Victoria and Western Australia, police are allowed to search a person who is reasonably believed to be in possession of an inhalant and confiscate it.

In England and Wales, it is illegal for retailers to sell volatile substances to anyone under the age of eighteen if there is reason to believe they will use it for inhalation and intoxication purposes.

There are no laws governing the sale or possession of inhalants in Canada. Alberta a western province of Canada however, has passed legislation prohibiting the sale of inhalant compounds to minors as well as the use of inhalants by minors.

As I have mentioned earlier there are no reliable data available to give a picture of the seriousness of the inhalant abuse problem in India. By the statistics available it is indeed saddening to know that India has maximum number of street children in the world. Since the street children are particularly vulnerable to nicotine abuse, inhalant abuse and drug dependence they contribute large numbers of inhalant abusers to the overall count.

Further there are no programs to identify, and provide interventions. Awareness generation has been taken up in some schools as it is estimated that a good number of school students experiment and are hooked onto inhalants along with nicotine, alcohol and/or cannabis. There are NGOs working with street children who provide awareness and medical cum counseling interventions where needed. However this is grossly inadequate.

The street children are a neglected lot and there are no concrete government policies to improve their condition. After lot of work has been done with street children to treat and rehabilitate them but they are back on the streets as there may not be a place to go to. We are then back to square one.

Despite this formidable picture of inhalant abuse in our country we have as yet not formulated plans or laws to tackle the menace.

There are no laws to curtail sale of inhalants, possession or abuse of inhalants in India.

The Narcotic Drugs and Psychotropic Substances Bill, 1985 was introduced in the Lok Sabha on 23 August 1985. It was passed by both the Houses of Parliament and it was assented by the President on 16 September 1985. It came into force on 14 November 1985 as THE NARCOTIC DRUGS AND PSYCHOTROPIC SUBSTANCES ACT, 1985 (shortened to NDPS Act). Under the NDPS Act, it is illegal for a person to produce/manufacture/cultivate, possess, sell, purchase, transport, store, and/or consume any narcotic drug or psychotropic substance.

Under one of the provisions of the act, the Narcotics Control Bureau was set up with effect from March 1986. The Act is designed to fulfill India's treaty obligations under the Single Convention on Narcotic Drugs, Convention on Psychotropic Substances, and United Nations Convention against Illicit Traffic in Narcotic Drugs and Psychotropic Substances. The Act has been amended three times - in 1988, 2001, and most recently in 2014.

The 2014 Amendment recognizes the need for pain relief as an important obligation of the government. It creates a class of medicines called Essential Narcotic Drugs (ENDs). Power for legislation on ENDs has been shifted from the state governments to the central governments so that the whole country now can have a uniform law covering these medicines which are needed for pain relief.

Subsequently, NDPS rules which would be applicable to all states and union territories has been announced by the government of India in May 2015. It also has included 6 drugs namely Morphine, Fentanyl, Methadone, Oxycodone, Codeine and Hydrocodone. According to these rules, there is a single agency - the state drug controller - who can approve recognized medical institutions (RMI) for stocking and dispensing ENDs, without the need for any other licenses. The RMIs are obliged to ensure proper documentation and to submit annual consumption statistics to the drug controller of the state.

The Act extends to the whole of India and it applies also to all Indian citizens outside India and to all persons on ships and aircraft registered in India.

There is a long list of drugs and medicines that fall under the NDPS umbrella and the act applies to all the drugs mentioned therein. *However inhalants have not been covered under the list.* There are some states that are in the process of devising laws which would help contain the inhalant sale and possession.

It has been found that whitener-inhaling addiction among the adolescent boys in Kerala is on the rise. The authorities say that it is mostly teens, youngsters in the age group of 13 and 17 years, who are the victims.

As part of a mission, the Narcotic Cell, Ernakulum, has filed a petition before the Sub-Divisional Magistrate, seeking a directive to ban the sale of products that contain intoxicating chemicals, like the whitener. Currently the law stipulates only the regulation of the sale of harmful solvent substances but the narcotic cell is seeking a directive to ban the sale of products (Joseph Saju, Assistant Commissioner of Police, Narcotic Cell, Ernakulum, Kerala).

However, they insist that parents and society should cooperate with them in this solvent abuse eradication mission. Unlike other drugs, curbing correction fluid abuse is difficult as even the parents are quite oblivious about the effect. The Narcotic cell, Ernakulum is therefore planning to conduct more seminars and counseling sessions about solvent abuse and also devising new ways to curb its use.

Apparently, a detailed examination conducted by the State Government Laboratory had also indicated that highly inflammable substances were found in adhesives and the same volatile aliphatic petroleum hydrocarbons were present in the whitener samples that were examined.

The Coimbatore general hospital registers and attends 8 to 10 patients of inhalant abuse every month. The trend is catching up with teenagers and adolescents.

A similar grim picture of inhalant abuse has been reported by NGOs working with street children in Kolkata, Mumbai and other metropolis.

The menace does not stop in big metropolis and is affecting small district towns as well now.

The Directorate of Education (DoE) has instructed schools to ban the use of correction fluids, whiteners and other substances. A circular, sent to schools on August 17, 2017, states that the DoE has banned the use of bottled correction fluids, thinners, whiteners, diluters and vulcanized solutions.

The circular from the department follows an order from the Juvenile Justice Board (JJB) in April this year asking the government to ban over-the-counter sale of such products to children less than 18 years to protect them from substance abuse. The JJB had said children should be allowed to buy correction fluids, whiteners, thinners and other such substances only if they are accompanied by parents or have a letter from school authorities instructing them to buy it.

In July this year, the Family and Health Department of the government also banned the sale of such products. Similar orders were issued in 2012 as well, by the then government.

School principals received the circular and forwarded the same to parents. "Shopkeepers too need to be made aware that they should not sell these products to children," said the principal of a south Delhi school. Many felt that implementing the order in government schools will be a bigger challenge as there are a large number of students. On the contrary, awareness generation programs in government run schools would give an opportunity to address a larger population about inhalants and make them equipped with knowledge.

In addition the mobilization of the media and the youth to spread awareness is the need of the hour. Media can reach far wider audiences and in a very short time. Youth represent the icon of health and fitness and can spread messages against drug/inhalant abuse to the younger generations.

Come what may but the menace has to be fought head-on and on a war footing.

CONCLUSION

Use of intoxication as a release from stress or for recreation has been an important part in the life of the human being and the society accepts this. There are traditional intoxicants (time tested as relatively safe for society) and traditional ways of taking it. This keeps the user and the social fabric safe. It is the untraditional substances as drugs and inhalants which have never been accepted as they destroy the human and the society.

You can count the number of drugs abused but counting the inhalants abused is simply out of our imagination. There happen to be over 15000 chemical compounds which are used in day to day life as ingredient of essential goods. These very compounds are also abused as inhalants by the drug dependent. The compounds that are being abused are increasing in numbers and newer ones are tried out, especially as the drug taking individual is ready to try out any chemical that comes his way in addition to what he may have already been using.

This untraditional intoxication has spread rapidly and the vulnerable targets are children and adolescents. It is rapidly devastating and only awareness about these compounds by all the people in society can safeguard the population more effectively.

The medical team is doing what it can do best. Treat. It can hold camps for awareness and treatment. Advise the policy makers for all that needs to be done.

The media can display, advertise, and have studio discussions to spread awareness about inhalant abuse. They can repeatedly reach millions in their persistent effort. School and university student awareness programs should be done regularly. NGOs can work along with the mainstream disciplines.

They have proven their unique place in being one of the bodies that offer their services even in the remotest areas where many can't reach. They can also work with the marginalized population of street children.

Besides awareness the laws can be devised to make sale of inhalants to minors an offence.

We are witnessing a time when the youngsters have unbridled energy and independence. They are self-willed and want to make their own decisions. Our responsibility is to equip them with proper knowledge about things so that they can save themselves and their dear ones from dangerously harmful enjoyments as the inhalants.

We are also witnessing a time when inhalants abuse and addiction is spreading amongst youngsters and children. One can foresee larger number falling prey to this addiction. School children are becoming very vulnerable, street children are the worst afflicted, call center workers, mechanics are other susceptible victims. The picture is becoming alarming rapidly and a timely action is a "war cry".

It may not be simple but it is a step in the right direction. The public involvement in this whole process can really make a big difference.

APPENDIX 1

PRESCRIPTION DRUGS – inducing DELIRIUM

1. Central acting agents
   - Sedative hypnotics (e.g., benzodiazepines)
   - Anticonvulsants (e.g., barbiturates)
   - Antiparkinsonian agents (e.g., benztropine, trihexyphenidyl)
2. Analgesics
   - Narcotics (meperidine)
   - Non-steroidal anti-inflammatory drugs*
3. Antihistamines (first generation hydroxyzine, diphenhydramine)
4. Gastrointestinal agents
   - Antispasmodics
   - H2-blockers*
5. Anti-nauseants
   - Scopolamine
   - Dimenhydrinate
6. Antibiotics
   - Fluoroquinolones*
7. Psychotropic medications
   - Tricyclic antidepressants
   - Lithium*

8. Cardiac medications

    - Antiarrhythmics

    - Digitalis*

    - Antihypertensives (b-blockers, methyldopa)

9. Miscellaneous

    - Skeletal muscle relaxants

    - Steroids

10. Liquid medications containing alcohol

11. Mandrax (Methaqualone)

12. Jimson weed (Datura stramonium) or the Devils weed.

13. Atropa belladonna extract (Datura plant extract)

APPENDIX 2

THE 12- STEP PROGRAM

Step 1: We admitted we were powerless over alcohol/drugs—that our lives had become unmanageable.

Step 2: Came to believe that a Power greater than we could restore us to sanity.

Step 3: Made a decision to turn our will and our lives over to the care of God as we understood Him.

Step 4: Made a searching and fearless moral inventory of ourselves.

Step 5: Admitted to God, to ourselves, and to another human being the exact nature of our wrongs.

Step 6: Were entirely ready to have God remove all these defects of character.

Step 7: Humbly asked Him to remove our shortcomings.

Step 8: Made a list of all persons we had harmed, and became willing to make amends to them all.

Step 9: Made direct amends to such people wherever possible, except when to do so would injure them or others.

Step 10: Continued to take personal inventory and when we were wrong promptly admitted it.

Step 11: Sought through prayer and meditation to improve our conscious contact with God, as we understood Him, praying only for knowledge of His will for us and the power to carry that out.

Step 12:   Having had a spiritual awakening as the result of these Steps, we tried to carry this message to alcoholics, and to practice these principles in all our affairs.

LIST OF
DE ADDICTION CENTERS

1. National Drug Dependence Treatment Centre, Ghaziabad, Uttar Pradesh. Ph: 0120-2788974. Open 24 hours.

2. Institute of Human Behavior & Allied Sciences, Dilshad Garden, New Delhi. Ph: 011-22112136

3. De-Addiction clinic, Department of Psychiatry, GB Pant Hospital, New Delhi. Ph: 011-23234242

4. De-Addiction Center, Department of Psychiatry, Dr R M L Hospital, New Delhi. Ph: 011-23365525

5. Department of Psychiatry, Safdarjung Hospital, New Delhi. Ph: 011-26198481

6. Sahyog Detox Centre run by the Deptt. Of Women & Child Development OHB-II Sewa Kutir, Delhi 110009. Admission through CWC.

7. Detox Centre for Beggars at Lampur Home, Delhi. (Run by Department of Social Welfare) (Admission through respective court)

Other De-Addiction centers

https://deaddictioncentres.in/services/free-treatment/

List of other government run and good private centers can be obtained from appropriate websites.

Organizations Working with Children

- UNICEF
- Save the Children
- Smile foundation
- Defence for children
- Child Rights and You (CRY)
- Red Cross Society
- Childs rights
- Salaam Balak Trust
- Seva Bharati
- Child fund

There are many more and one could refer to the websites for such organizations.

REFERENCES

1. Indian J Psychiatry. 2016 Jan-Mar; 58(1): 93–96.

   doi: 10.4103/0019-5545.174396, PMCID: PMC4776591, PMID: 26985113

   Drinking habits in ancient India

   Ottilingam Somasundaram, D. Vijaya Raghavan, and A. G. Tejus Murthy

2. The Huffington Post, February 2015

   Humans Have Been Getting High since Prehistoric Times, Research Shows

   Macrina Cooper White.

3. UNODC bulletin on Narcotics. Issue 3-001, 1957.

   United Nations Office on Drugs and Crime.

   Abolition of Opium use in India.

4. U Chicago Medicine, Communications, May 2005

   As morphine turns 200, drug that blocks its side effects reveals new secrets

5. Behavioral Brain Research. Volume 277, 15 January 2015, Pages 146–192

   Special Issue: Serotonin Review the role of serotonin in drug use and addiction

   ChristianP.Müllera, Judith R. Homberg

6. Trends Mol Med. 2008 Aug; 14(8): 341–350. Published online 2008 Jul 16. doi:

    10.1016/j.molmed.2008.06.004 PMCID: PMC275337 NIHMSID: NIHMS126270

    PMID: 18635399

    Epigenetic mechanisms in drug addiction, William Renthal and Eric J. Nestler

7. National Inhalant Prevention Coalition – Newsletter update 2018

8. The Big Book of Alcoholics Anonymous

9. Goodenough book on Draw a Person Test

DISCLAIMER

The author has taken all the care to be exact in details. In the ever changing research some facts change over time. The author does not take responsibility for these. The reader is advised to consult or inform the author for any such facts. The book is meant to spread awareness of inhalant abuse and its treatment. It should be of great help to students, parents, teachers, doctors, psychologist and the general public.

Author Email: sanjeevprasad.psy@gmail.com